Testimonials

Following our series of sessions with The Phone Lady, we experienced a 25% lift in our small business advisors' ability to convert messages to returned phone calls, and phone conversations to appointments. In addition, everyone received a confidence boost in terms of their telephone communication skills. Working with The Phone Lady has been very effective for us.
Natacha Lemay-Reaume, Senior Manager, Small Business Banking , Ontario North East & Atlantic Canada, TD Bank Group

Excellent pace and content. Delivered at the right level for a diverse audience. Good preparation to suit our needs, not a canned presentation.
Scott Allan, Owner, Apple Self Storage

The straight forward, no nonsense delivery and interaction was easy to take. Three hours can be a long time to maintain a group's focus but that did not happen. The group was genuinely engaged throughout.
Bill VanGenne, Technical Services Manager, Arrow Construction Products

I've been a fan of The Phone Lady for a number of years and have recently had the pleasure of making use of her services! Mary Jane's compassionate approach helped me unearth the source of my phone fears, discover wording to help alleviate them and learn strategies to complete successful cold calls with new found confidence! Thank you ever so much for your help—your impact is truly lasting and I call on your words of wisdom as regular reminders when phone intimidation strikes!
Lorelei Phillips, Opportunities Liaison, L7 Opportunities Consulting

I enjoyed this workshop very much. I thought that Mary Jane was very knowledgeable and had many tips and suggestions that will help me out with customers on the phone as well as the difficult calls that we sometimes have to deal with. She was very respectful and courteous while ensuring that we were at ease and I would highly recommend this workshop to anyone who deals with customer service on the phones. Thank you, Mary Jane, for a job well done.
Crystal Jamieson, Advertising, Times & Transcript

Your stories make everything come to life. You're a wonderful speaker!
Teresa Wilkins, Service Specialist, Johnson Inc.

You, Mary Jane, were simply amazing. I appreciated your being so personable and approachable. Your information is invaluable! I'm looking forward to implementing all I've gleaned from you today.
Dinah Wray, Site Manager, Apple Self Storage

Very informative. Easy to visualize. Relevant to our roles.
Colleen Warren, Operations Manager, Johnson Inc.

A great workshop! I learned so much from this that I am actually looking forward to calling existing and potential clients. I really enjoyed how you cater to individual questions and to general situations that can be applied to all.
Ryan Meaney, Owner, Halifax Hype

It's not often I walk away from a training session and wish it had been longer. Great substance developed in a professional manner.
James Stephen, Sales Manager, Grand Cayman Marriott Beach Resort

A great day, very informative. I look forward to creating a "wow" experience over the phone. Great tips for improvement!
Trena Crewe, Director, Donor Relations, IWK Health Centre
Foundation

An excellent course! Taught me what I can do, and will do, to differentiate myself and the hotels I represent from our competition. Pace was good. Mary Jane is very engaging. Highly recommended for anyone who spends a large portion of their day on the phone.
Sherrie Fortier, Business Development Sales Manager, Marriott
Hotels & Resorts Canada

The Phone Book

Essential Telephone Communication Skills

Pick it Up &
Make Things Happen!

Mary Jane Copps

Boularderie
Island Press

Cover Layout by ON TIME Design harvegrant@gmail.com
Chart Page 98-99 courtesy Daley Progress www.daleyprogress.com
Back cover author photo by Rebecca Clarke www.rebeccaclarke.ca
Credit for *The Phone Lady* logo: Jay Hiltz, Partner & Creative Director, Kohoot Media http://kohoot.com/

Library and Archives Canada Cataloguing in Publication

Copps, Mary Jane, 1958-, author
      The phone book : essential telephone communication skills / Mary Jane Copps.

Includes bibliographical references.
ISBN 978-0-9918552-8-5 (pbk.)

      1. Telephone selling. 2. Business communication. I. Title.

HF5438.3.C662 2015   658.85   C2014-904587-5

www.thephonelady.com

A Boularderie Island Press Publication
www.boularderieislandpress.com

Printed in Canada

Table of Contents

This book is dedicated to:

Janet E. Bardon, for helping me discover the word "just" on the phone;

Sean McDermott, for insisting that I share the telephone skill set;

and

Jay Hiltz, who's logo design brought *The Phone Lady* to life.

Phone Phobia

The majority of people dislike making phone calls. Why? They believe that as soon as they dial a number, something dreadful is going to happen, such as they'll:

- Say the wrong thing
- Stumble when leaving a message
- Be laughed at or thought foolish by the person they are calling
- Be unable to answer a question
- Say someone's name incorrectly or forget a person's name
- Be treated with anger or disrespect
- Lose their voice
- Forget why they called and what they want to say
- Speak at length with the wrong person
- Have the other person hang up on them
- Be unable to connect with the right person
- Run into a "gatekeeper", a receptionist or assistant that insists they leave a message
- And I'm sure there's more!

Any one or combination of these reasons can result in phone phobia (a documented social phobia similar to the fear of public speaking) or something most sales managers are well acquainted with—call reluctance. I've seen these conditions in action throughout my career.

Working as a real estate manager in my early 20's, I saw that agents who didn't pick up the phone had listings that took longer to sell—or didn't have any listings at all.

In my first job as a journalist, I was the one that ended up with all the stories involving phone calls to famous or high-profile people; everyone else was too uncomfortable. But these were the stories that got on the front page and advanced my career.

Later when I worked for a large magazine publisher, I witnessed the high turnover in sales departments. If someone sold advertising and hesitated to pick up the phone they didn't last very long.

And then, when I owned my first company, I watched staff members think of and act on every excuse possible to avoid making a phone call. It drove me crazy.

If you recognize your own behaviour here, what can you do? How can you leap over your fear and get on with the task?

Well, I believe you can't "leap" over it. Getting past fear, or habitual reluctance, takes time, commitment and discipline. There's no easy way, no magic solution. I know this from experience.

It took me almost six years to conquer my biggest—and most life-limiting—fear. The process involved a series of small steps and a lot of setbacks.

Five years before I was born, an accident took place that had a huge impact on my life. A truck carrying long metal rods came to a sudden stop in front of the car my dad was driving. One of the rods went through the windshield on the passenger side and almost through my mom's eye into her skull. The near-death experience left her with an obvious scar near her eyebrow…and a tremendous fear of cars and traffic.

This fear was passed along to me through her behaviour in the car on our many (too many!) family trips from Northern Ontario to Toronto, Montreal, all kinds of places we shouldn't have gone with a terrified, eventually screaming, woman in the front seat.

For some unknowable reason, this didn't impact my ability to be a trusting passenger, but it did prevent me from driving a car.

When I was 20 I took a driving course in Toronto. I had a lovely instructor. His name was Burton; he was funny and kind. When I think back on that experience I can say for sure that I didn't know I was afraid — I only knew that when Burton was no longer in the car with me, when an examiner sat in that passenger seat, I couldn't drive. Burton took me to get my driver's license five times. The fifth examiner looked me in the eye and said *"Some people are too nervous and aren't meant to drive."* I believed him.

And for the 20 years I lived in Toronto, with its excellent public transit system and family and friends who were willing to serve as the occasional chauffer, not driving wasn't much of an issue, but then I moved to the smaller city of Halifax and not having a driver's license was a serious liability.

My patient, kind husband volunteered to teach me how to drive. We had only been together three years and he really didn't know what he was getting himself into. To be honest, I didn't know either. I didn't know that over the years the fear had strengthened, expanded, became a monolith. That first Sunday morning I drove approximately 200 meters on a deserted stretch of road before I pulled over and wept uncontrollably. That's fear!

It took almost six years (seriously, I went and wrote the test for my beginners' license FIVE times), hundreds of emotional outbursts and a month of lessons with a caring, knowledgeable driving instructor to finally get my license.

A series of small steps—that's what it took for me to conquer my fear and realize—I'm a good driver.

And you are a good communicator on the telephone, you simply don't know it yet. But here's how you can find out:

1

Identify your motivation for tackling your phone fear.
Not having a driver's license in Nova Scotia meant saying "no" to client projects, not attending events, and relying on other people a lot of the time to pick me up and drive me home. How is your phone fear impacting you, your career, your finances, your family?

I need to communicate effectively on the telephone because:

✓

_____

_____

_____

_____

2

Make the commitment. Tell yourself—and keep telling yourself—that you choose to eliminate fear from your life. If you choose not to pick up the phone, that's different from being afraid to pick up the phone.

> I, _____ commit to becoming an effective communicator on the phone. ✓

3

Tell the truth. For years and years I told myself—and others—that I didn't drive a car in order to save money, protect the environment, stay fit. That wasn't the truth. I was only able to challenge my fear when I admitted it existed. Be honest about your "why" for not picking up the phone.

> The reason(s) I hesitate to pick up the phone are: ✓

_____

_____

_____

_____

_____

4

Tell others about your fear—and your plans to conquer it. Much to my surprise, when I finally started talking about my fear, I discovered lots of people shared it. Many people are terrified of driving a car. Discovering this played an important role in my taking on the challenge—and it will for you too. Trust me, there are lots—and lots—of people who fear the phone.

> *I have told these people about my reluctance to pick up the phone:*
>
> ✓
>
> _____
> _____
> _____
> _____
> _____

5

Find a buddy, someone who will gently hold you accountable and celebrate all of your successes, even the small ones. My husband was my buddy. The amount of time he devoted to helping me and his genuine enthusiasm for each small step along the way...I wouldn't have the driver's license without his cheerleading and support.

> *These friends have agreed to be my telephone "buddies":*
>
> ✓
>
> _____
> _____
> _____
> _____
> _____

6

Find a coach, *a person that understands your fear and knows the path you need to take to leave it behind. Allow them to help you craft and practice your phonework. For me it was an amazing driving instructor named Robie. Just thinking about him makes me smile. Every time I drive the car I hear his voice in my head and I laugh at the number of times he said to me "Now we're going to do something you're really going to hate, but you'll be fine."*

_____ has agreed to be my coach as I work towards becoming an effective communicator on the telephone. ✓

7

Give yourself deadlines. *When do you want to be fluent and comfortable on the phone? Who do you want to call? Is there an event, a promotion, a commission on which you can set your aim? Deadlines keep us motivated.*

I want to be fluent and comfortable on the phone by _____ so that I can: ✓

_____

_____

_____

_____

_____

8

Celebrate every success, no matter how small. The first time I drove the car without any tears, we celebrated. The first time I made a left-hand turn without instruction, we celebrated. Each step you take towards your goal is important. Acknowledge it.

Yeah for me! These accomplishments are leading me to become an effective communicator on the phone:

✓

_____

_____

_____

_____

_____

So, what's next?

Start learning the skill set in an environment that's comfortable for you. In other words, phoning the CEO of a multi-national corporation without any preparation or study is not the way to overcome phone fear.

Once you understand the skill set, then you do need to practice—a lot. Picking up the phone once a month won't dissolve your fear and discomfort. (Like many new drivers, I started out in large empty parking lots and then moved to weekly 6 am Sunday morning drives.)

As you practice your phone skills, perhaps with friends and colleagues to start, you'll realize that the scenarios that frightened you, held you back, don't happen. You won't forget what to say. You won't lose your voice. No one will hang up on you. And each successful call you make will alleviate more and more of your fear until one day you pick up the phone and speak with confidence to a total stranger.

Just like me…I don't accidentally drive on the wrong side of the road, or put my foot on the gas instead of the brake, or scrape adjacent cars in parking lots, or miss seeing pedestrians. In fact, I even know how to drive a car when the brakes fail! Turns out I'm a very good driver—something I should have found out about myself years ago.

Conquering fear is an experience like no other. You will feel liberated; you'll have a surge of confidence in all areas of your life. Banishing something that once controlled you is incredibly powerful.

I believe that everyone has the ability to communicate on the phone effectively; I know that it's an important, valuable life skill. Developing this skill does require some knowledge—which is the purpose of this book—and some practice. The practice part is up to you; knowledge begins on the next page.

Did you know?

Overwhelm is a word we hardly used at all until a few years ago. Now we hear it all the time. You'll ask people how they are and they'll say "I'm completely overwhelmed." The word originated in the early 14th century and is actually a combination of the word "over" and the Middle English word "whelmen" which means "to turn upside down". It is thought to have been a reference to sailing i.e. being washed over by a big wave.

Common definitions include:
1) drown or bury beneath a huge mass;
2) completely defeat;
3) inundate.

Our ability to communicate successfully on the phone today directly relates to our ability to understand, empathize with and navigate the fact that everyone we are calling is overwhelmed.

This is Intimate Communication

2

The telephone offers us the ability to create intimate and detailed conversations with our clients, prospects, employers—and family and friends—because, at its essence, the phone is a distraction-free medium. What does this mean, exactly?

Well, first let's compare phone conversations to face-to-face events, like networking, meetings, even dinner parties. I often struggle at networking events because I'm so easily distracted by movement. I'll look up as new people arrive or leave, totally abandoning the person who's speaking to me, making them feel like I'm searching for someone more interesting. Often at meetings I'll start following my own thoughts about an issue and tune out the discussion that surrounds me. When I rejoin the conversation, everyone has moved on to a new topic. And large dinner parties can make me nervous. I will try to focus on the conversation to my right, but tidbits of the conversation on my left or across the table will enter my consciousness and I'll want to join in. I'll lose my train of thought and appear downright rude.

None of these things happen when I talk on the phone.

When I communicate by email there are different distractions. I'm actually a big fan of email, coming as I do from an era where direct mail involved colourful brochures, typewritten envelopes, stamps and a trip to the post office. And then waiting 10 days or more before following up. Believe me, I remain amazed and indebted to the grace and speed of email but compared to the phone....

Writing takes longer than talking and then I have to wait for a response. Sometimes I have more questions when the reply arrives and there's another delay. And then there's misunderstandings that occur because I've misread someone's meaning or implied a tone that wasn't intended. And often, if I receive a really long email message, I simply don't give it my full attention. There are too many messages to read and too much work to do.

None of these things happen when I talk on the phone.

Here's how I learned the power and importance of focus on the phone:

By the mid-90's I'd already been selling on the phone all day, everyday for seven years. My close ratio was good and no matter what, our company could count on my ability to produce revenue. But my neck and shoulders were extremely unhappy. My youngest stepdaughter, Nina, organized a rescue effort in the form of a headset. I was thrilled. I remember very clearly taking it out of its box, reading all the instructions, setting it up, making a few test calls to check the volume and then...getting back to work.

Those first few calls felt very strange. My hands were awkward, like the wings of a baby bird. I didn't know what to do with them. I'd always used both of them for every phone call—holding the phone in my left hand and using my right hand to take notes or to cup the mouthpiece in order to soften background noise.

I didn't yet have a computer on my desk, but my hands found paperwork. After I dialed a number, I'd start sorting or reading or writing as the call went through. Can you guess what happened?

My success rate dropped dramatically and my faltering performance impacted morale throughout the office. Also, my conversations were no longer enjoyable—they had a sputtering, uneven quality. I was loathe to give up the expensive headset, so I persevered for two weeks and then...unplugged. Within days all was well, my numbers were back up, the conversations were interesting and fun, everyone was relieved.

While I do work with a headset today (that technology has improved dramatically) I still approach phone calls with a deep respect for the importance of focus—and I encourage you to do the same.

When we do other things while we are on the phone we become distracted and this is evident in the sound of our voice. The person we are calling hears that they are not important, that they are simply a task in our day, and this does not inspire conversation. Distraction also takes away from our ability to truly listen, to "hear" the needs, questions and comments of our clients, prospects, employers. Our job on the phone is to provide information, be a problem solver, and how can we do that if we are unable to listen?

The first step to becoming a great communicator on the telephone is eliminating distraction when you are making and receiving calls. For myself this means having a door I can close or perhaps facing away from an open door to avoid being distracted by the movement of others in the office. I also either turn off my computer monitor or look away from it, so that I'm not tempted to check, file or write email. And I always have a pen and paper nearby. Having a pen in our hand ignites our creative brain and helps us be more responsive to what we hear. It also allows us to jot notes to ourselves so we can keep listening and not interrupt the speaker.

You may need to do other things in order to engage in distraction-free phone communication. For example, my husband has to walk around while he's talking on the phone. The movement helps him focus and listen.

What do you need to do to be distraction free while on the phone?

> *I can create distraction-free phone conversations by:* ✓

_____

_____

_____

_____

_____

Did you know?

Calling by number was not introduced until 1884, and then only in large centres, so that at first operators had to memorize the names, addresses and telephone numbers of all persons in the exchange area.

A caller rang "Central" and waited for the operator to give a short ring back, letting them know she was available. The caller said, "Give me John Jones". The operator countered, "Which John Jones? The one on Jarvis Street or the one on Sherbourne Street?"

FROM: The First Century of Service - Bell 1880-1980
Private Printing by Bell, Montreal, 1980, Bell Canada Archives doc. no. 25461

Review Notes

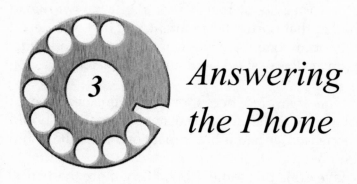

Answering the Phone

The phone skill that creates the biggest and most long-lasting impression is also the one we tend to neglect—answering the phone. More often than not, we approach it as an interruption in our day instead of an introduction to an important and valuable conversation.

Take for example a phone call I had with a new business acquaintance. We had met at a networking event and were moving towards working on a project together. There was a delay in my receiving some information and the aim of my phone call was to discover if there was something I needed to do to move things along.

I experienced that moment of relief and joy in the initial seconds of her answering the phone. "Hooray," I thought to myself. "This is going to get done today." But then the sound of her voice changed everything, not only for the phone conversation but for our relationship.

She was, well, miserable. It's hard for me to choose the right adjectives but they would be something like frustrated, angry, impatient, unwelcoming. You get the idea.

If she had sounded panicked, I would have said *"It sounds like I've caught you at an inconvenient time. I'll call back tomorrow."* But it wasn't panic and I felt myself struggle. Briefly I thought it was about me, something I had done that was causing her reaction. Instead of backing out of the call, I forged ahead in search of some clarity.

In the end it wasn't about me. It was about her workload and the fact that, at that particular moment, she had no interest in talking to me, or anyone else. She was dismissive and rude, although did manage to say she'd send me what I needed as soon as possible.

In the way she answered her phone, this businesswoman inadvertently shared with me an aspect of her personality I should never have experienced. It had a big impact on our relationship in that...we don't have a relationship.

Most of us have done this same thing, likely more than once. We answer the phone behaving as if the caller can see us, can see that we are trying to finish an email, or rushing to a meeting, or about to enjoy our lunch. Our "hello" is filled with a frustration and annoyance that is startling and, more importantly, damaging to our relationships with colleagues, customers, prospects and potential employers.

So how do we prevent this from happening? Follow these five simple rules for answering your phone and you'll always create a positive impression:

1 Answer Between The Second And Third Ring

Every phone call is an interruption. We are not sitting at our desks waiting for phone calls—we're busy. So when the phone does ring and we answer it immediately, we have the sound of interruption in our voice. It can be heard by the caller as frustration, annoyance, impatience, even anger.

Instead of grabbing for the phone instantly, use the first ring to stop what you are doing. Take your hands off your keyboard, put down your pen, push aside your sandwich and acknowledge that you are about to answer the phone and that you want to create a positive impression.

On the second ring, smile. I know this sounds trite but in reality, the muscles we use to smile impact the sound of our voice. It is next to impossible to sound frustrated or impatient while you are smiling.

Then, before the third ring, pick up the phone and welcome your caller.

2 Visualize The Caller As If She Is Standing In Front Of You

When we meet a customer, prospect or employer face-to-face, we are warm and welcoming. It doesn't even cross our mind to be impatient or frustrated. We shake hands, introduce ourselves and give them our full attention. And this is exactly how we should behave on the phone.

You wouldn't shake hands with someone and withhold your name would you? Answering the phone with your name creates "welcome" and puts the caller at ease. Make sure you say your name slowly and clearly, at the same speed you use when you shake hands with someone.

27

3 Express Your Desire To Be Of Service

When we answer our phone we want to let the caller know they have our full attention, that we are interested in hearing what they have to say and in having a conversation. Once we have mastered smiling and creating our welcoming tone of voice, we want to choose the best words to express our desire to be of service.

For everyone these words will be slightly different. Here is how I answer my phone:

"Mary Jane speaking. How can I help you?"

I don't use a company name because I am the company and the phone is my direct line. When *The Phone Lady* grows and has a general office number, then I would answer like this:

"The Phone Lady. Mary Jane speaking. How can I help

you?"

I tend to use only my first name for two reasons:

1) it is already two words and that seems long enough to me; and 2) it is less formal, more open and friendly.

The words you choose will depend on your company, its branding and relationship with its clients.

While seeking employment, make sure you answer the phone with your full name. You want the caller to be confident they've reached the right candidate. And make sure your voice contains energy and enthusiasm. No one wants to interview someone who's bored and tired.

Design a greeting that isn't too long (this causes callers some frustration) and uses words that you find easy to say (won't cause you to stumble). Here's another example, appropriate perhaps for a hotel or restaurant: *"Welcome to The Phone Lady. Mary Jane speaking. How can I help you today?"*

4 Slow Down And Enunciate

We've all had it happen. We've called somewhere and the person answering the phone speaks so quickly we have no idea if we've reached the right number. It makes for a rough start to a conversation.

Speak each word separately. Rushing pushes the words together and causes confusion, especially around your name. On two occasions I obviously spoke too fast when leaving a message. One person returned my call and asked for Mary Jacobs (which means I rushed together "Jane" and "Copps") and one asked for Mary Jane Poppins (not sure how that happened).

5 *If You Can't Be Welcoming Don't Answer*

Regardless of my rules, sometimes a phone call arrives at exactly the wrong moment. You are late for a meeting, your printer just ran out of ink, you can't find your car keys and…the phone rings. No matter how hard you try, it is unlikely you'll get frustration and impatience out of your voice, and certainly you won't be able to focus on the caller. Rather than create a negative impression, allow the call to go to voicemail. Used correctly, voicemail offers a valuable opportunity to make a great impression. Keep reading to find out more!

When I answer my phone, I will welcome callers with this message:

_____

_____

_____

_____

_____

Did you know?

About 103 million telephone conversations are held in this country every day—an annual total of about 34 billion—more than twice the number of all letters, post cards and telegrams combined. This enormous and growing use of the telephone makes it more important than ever, that everyone, especially those in business, should know how to use the service with greatest profit to themselves.

The telephone provides communication by voice— the natural and quickest way of making your thoughts and personality known to others. You like to deal by telephone with people whose voices and manner of speaking show them to be courteous, interested, alert.

Every time you telephone you make a definite impression—good, bad, or indifferent—on the person at the other end, just as surely as you get an idea of what that person is like. Your voice, what you say, and how you say it, is what reveals you to others. It's on just such impressions that much of this country's business depends; for if favorable they make for confidence and good will.

From: You and Your Telephone, A Pamphlet on Good Telephone Usage, New York Telephone Company, 1941, Bell Canada Archives, Telephone Etiquette file

Your Voicemail Messages

4

When you are unable to answer your phone, do you have a receptionist that creates a positive impression with the caller? For most of you the answer to this question is "no". And even if you do have a full-time receptionist, calls that come in for you are likely directed to your voicemail.

So, when someone reaches your voicemail, what do they hear? They should hear your desire to be of service but in most cases they listen to one of the following:

The Flight Attendant

This message has the same intonation and pacing as the safety procedure instructions delivered at the beginning of every flight. It is well rehearsed; it contains no errors or "um's" or "ah's". It is absolutely professional—but lacks all trace of warmth, interest and personality. Callers certainly receive information but are left feeling like the person they called is impersonal and cold.

The Indy Driver

This message whizzes along at top speed. The words are spoken so quickly, fit together so tightly, they create a visual of the person taking one big breath and talking until they can't breathe any more. It gives the impression of rush and stress — someone who is too busy to engage with callers. Rather than a welcome, this message pushes people away.

The Minimalist

Efficiency is valuable and we all admire people who get to the point, but being greeted by *"Jane Smith's office. Leave a message,"* creates doubt. Does this Jane Smith still work for the company? Does she pick up messages? Am I calling the right person, the right organization? Where there is doubt, there is a caller that goes elsewhere for what they need.

The Detailer

I am a strong advocate of the dated message—as you are soon to find out—but not the play-by-play of one's entire schedule, and an optional phone number, and a website address, and a bit of information about tomorrow's schedule ... you know what I mean. The goal of a great voicemail message is to let a caller know you can be of service, not that you are constantly being of service to others.

Eeyore

For anyone not familiar with Winnie the Pooh, Eeyore is the stuffed donkey in the stories and he's generally characterized as gloomy and pessimistic. In animated versions his voice is low and slow and...tired and bored. The business world is full of voicemail messages that sound like Eeyore. What a caller hears is someone who has no interest at all in the job or the company. This not only pushes them towards the competition, it shuts the door behind them as they go.

Know that your voicemail is your receptionist. In fact, it's your avatar. It represents you each and every time someone reaches it ... and they do make decisions based on what they hear. It is important that you create a welcoming, dynamic voicemail message.

Here's how:

1 Use the notion of a real-person receptionist as your guideline. If you had someone answering the phone for you, how would you instruct them to greet each caller? What information would they provide?

2 Most of us have experienced reaching voicemail and doubting that our message will be received by anyone. Something about the content and/or the tone of voice makes us question that the person really exists. This can be avoided by creating the daily message. While I know that many of you will groan at the thought, having a message that says *"It's Monday September 21 and you've reached the office of Mary Jane Copps..."* lets callers know I am working today, I want to connect with them today, I am thinking about them and their needs today.

3 If it's a challenge to create a daily message, consider doing one for the week. This will at least prevent callers from hearing the same message over and over and over and... .

4 Record your message the night before. In order to maintain the discipline, I create mine every night before I go to bed. In the morning our voices can sound dry and scratchy. Also, it's not difficult to fall behind schedule in the morning and forget to change your message. Or perhaps drink too much coffee and then record your message at top speed.

5 Breath deeply before you start to record and make sure you smile. This will allow your voice to sound calm, happy and welcoming.

6 Keep the message brief. You don't have to include every detail of your day. You do want callers to know about your availability and when they can expect a return call. For example *"I'm in meetings throughout the day today but am checking voicemail when possible. I will return your call."*

7 Allow your message to work for you as well as your clients and prospects. For example, by telling callers *"I'm delivering workshops throughout the day today but will return all calls tomorrow"*, I can focus on the clients in front of me while still communicating with my callers.

8 When you do need to provide an alternate contact phone number—perhaps to another member of your team, or to your cell phone, make sure you say the number at the same speed it takes you to write it down, and then repeat it so your caller can verify they've written it down correctly.

9 If possible, use a land line to create your message. Cell phones are prone to producing echoes, static and even unintentional silence.

10 Check your message. While it sounded good to you while you were recording it, the reality may be that the dog barked in the background, or your volume was too low, or you did have too much coffee.

The Vacation Message

There are many, many people who do a great job of creating warm, welcoming and informative voicemail messages until ... they go on vacation. I'm assuming it is the excitement of taking time off work that suddenly makes people...thoughtless.

I do empathize. There's nothing like that last day of work before a holiday, the focus we have as we "tie up loose ends" and that moment when we're ready to walk out the door, embrace our well-earned time off. And I'm guessing it's at this moment, the one just seconds away from freedom, when we remember to change our voicemail message. More than any other message, the vacation message is delivered at the speed of light, often impossible to understand and lacks any valuable information.

Here's some tips for creating a helpful, personable vacation message:

1 Skip all the dates. You know what I mean..."*I'm on vacation from...through to...*" It causes confusion. Instead simply state when you will be back at work, i.e. "*I'll be back at my desk on Monday July 30 ... .*"

2 Be honest. You are going on vacation and you deserve to enjoy it without work interruptions. We all deserve this and it's essential to our health and our creativity. So there's no value in saying you are monitoring and returning messages; I know it's unlikely you are going to call me back.

3 Speak slowly—and repeat. Many vacation messages include the option to contact someone else, which is great customer service. But it's totally defeated if the information is given so quickly that neither name nor phone number can be understood. As a rule, we are not prepared to "take a message" when we make outbound calls. Take this into consideration, stating names and phone numbers slowly and clearly, at the same speed it would take you to write them down. Then say them again so your caller can check what they've written down.

4 Sound happy. After all, while I'm listening to your message you are on vacation.

Finally, it's important to recognize that sometimes it is your company's telephone equipment that's impacting voicemail messages. If you are in sales or customer service and know that the equipment is an issue, speak up. If you are in management, consider the following:

1 Check the menus on your phone equipment regularly, at least every quarter. Is everyone on staff listed? Are people listed that no longer work for the company? Who is monitoring messages for those that have left recently or are away on leave?

2 Many companies set up their voicemail system based on what they need, what will be convenient for them. But it needs to be convenient for customers and prospects too. It's always worth contacting a few clients and getting feedback on their experiences with your phone system.

3 Do you get frustrated with your own system? If you do, chances are your customers are frustrated too. Do something to change it.

Sample Messages

"For Monday September 8th you've reached the office of Mary Jane Copps. Sorry I've missed your call. I am in meetings this morning but at my desk this afternoon. Do please leave a message. I will return your call. Thank you."

Design your daily message here:

✓

_____

_____

_____

_____

_____

"You've reached the office of Mary Jane Copps. I am currently enjoying my niece's wedding in Mexico but I'll be back at my desk on March 24th. I will return your call at that time. If you need a response before March 24th, indicate that in your message and my assistant, Joanne, will contact you promptly. Thank You."

Design your vacation message here:

✓

_____

_____

_____

_____

_____

Did you know?

The first sound-proof telephone booths were introduced by The Bell Telephone Company of Canada in 1898. Early booths were often impressive affairs equipped with writing desk, rug and silk curtains. Some persons mistook them for elevators. Before folding doors were introduced, the double doors of the booth sometimes stuck, and telephone users had to fight to get out.

***

Current events often had an impact on telephone service. For example in 1900 it was reported that "One hundred and thirty-three business firms in Toronto have been asked to have their telephones closed down for two hours so that telephone operators might watch the parade of soldiers returning from the Boer War."

FROM: The First Century of Service - Bell 1880-1980
Private Printing by Bell, Montreal, 1980, Bell Canada Archives doc. no. 25461

Review Notes

Leaving
Messages

Leaving messages is an important part of phone communication, especially when your call relates to sales, customer service or a job search.

Here's why:

1 Most people view call display before listening to their messages. Many take note of the difference between calls received and messages left. Any phone number appearing regularly in call display without a matching message is perceived as either aggressive (i.e. aggressive salesperson) or unimportant (if it was urgent, you'd leave a message). It's unlikely that a call from that number will ever be answered. The same holds true for all calls that appear as "Blocked" or "Unknown".

2 Hanging up is still considered rude. While this may change in the future, right now etiquette dictates that you leave a message even if it's as simple as *"Mary Jane Copps calling. Sorry I missed you. I'll try back later today."*

3 We can never know for sure how our actions impact others and I'm grateful that workshop participants have shared these two possibilities: a) as a survivor of domestic abuse, calls with no message attached cause fear, stress and panic; b) as a mother of traveling children, a call with no message inspires visions of accidents, hospitals, emergencies, etc. Leaving a message is an easy way to avoid creating emotional distress.

4 Your message is a marketing tool. The words you say and how you say them do have an impact and support both building relationships and creating a strong brand.

It's important to understand that leaving a message has a lot in common with giving a short speech. Combine this with that fact that it's being recorded and it's no wonder we often get nervous or tongue-tied at "the sound of the tone".

The key to success is the same as with public speaking— preparation. When we leave a rambling, detailed and confused message for someone, it's usually because we didn't give any forethought to what we wanted to say or accomplish. Avoiding this is as simple as writing down the points you want to include so you stay focused, and continually practicing your well-crafted message.

A well-crafted message has three components:

First...

It's easy to understand and write down. You want to follow guidelines similar to those for creating your voicemail message. Slow down when you say your name and make sure you enunciate. No mumbling allowed. And don't rush through your phone number. A good rule to follow is saying your phone number at the same speed it takes you to write it down. Even after almost three decades on the phone, I still reach for a piece of scrap paper from time to time and write down my number as I leave a message. If I can write it down, then so can the person I'm calling. By repeating your phone number a second time, they are able to verify what they've written down. Everyone reverses numbers occasionally.

Second...

It inspires a return call. The majority of the time when we leave a message, we want that person to call us back. And in an ideal world, that's exactly what would happen. But remember "overwhelmed"? Everyone we are calling has too much to do and often struggles to decide which calls they have time to return.

For example, I spent several years working with the Vice-President of Regional Marketing for a large chain of drug stores. This is a BIG job. It involves tons of meetings, lots of travel (the need to visit each store during the course of the year) and multiple decisions every day, everything from artwork to hiring to event planning and beyond. And of course, she was doing important things outside her job, like raising a young family and looking after elderly relatives. So early on in our relationship she requested that most of our communication take place by email, and that was very straightforward.

But one day something came across my desk that I knew was too difficult to clearly explain in an email and I called her. She did return my call that same day but when I answered my phone she said "Hi Mary Jane, it's Suzanne from ABC Company. I've got 5 minutes to return 50 calls. Talk fast."

This wasn't rude; it gave me a visual of her very busy life which I use every time I leave a message for anyone—and which I get to share with you. Know that the people you are calling may be travelling for days or weeks at a time, a situation that isn't conducive to taking the time to return calls. Or they are going from meeting to meeting to meeting, with little time to even check voicemail regularly.

Here's a message that works: *"Hi Suzanne, it's Mary Jane calling from The Phone Lady. I have one quick question for you. I'm at my desk today until 5 pm. You can reach me at 1-877-404-3290. That's 1-877-404-3290. Thanks."*

Indicating that you have only "one" question that's going to be "quick" does help busy people decide they can return your call. Also, the message doesn't contain a lot of detail. When we're busy, listening to lots of detail isn't possible. We often fast forward to the end, save the message and then...get back to it in days or weeks or not at all.

Third...

It eliminates phone tag. While voicemail is a tremendous convenience, it brings with it the annoyance of phone tag—the endless back and forth of messages between two people who don't connect in real time. Often, when they do finally reach each other, frustration colours the beginning of the conversation.

To avoid this situation, always leave details about when you are available to receive a return call and let them know when you will call again. Here's an example: *"Hi David. It's Mary Jane from The Phone Lady. I have one quick question for you regarding next week's workshop. I'm at my desk today until 4:30 pm and you can reach me at 1-877-404-3290. That's 1-877-404-3290. If we don't connect by 4:30 today, know that I'll try you back again tomorrow afternoon."*

This message shows a lot of respect for David's time. If he picks up the message after 4:30, he knows not to call, and he knows when I'm going to call again. If he's available the next afternoon, he'll keep an eye out for my call. I've also learned that mentioning I'm going to call again inspires return calls. David listens to the message and thinks "Hmmm, well if she's going to keep calling I might as well get back to her."

Voicemail and email can also create a great partnership. If you are not already regularly communicating with someone by email, a phone message prior to hitting "send" is very helpful. For example: *"Hi David. It's Mary Jane calling from The Phone Lady. You and I met last week in Toronto and I said I'd send you more information on my workshops. I'm sending that to you by email today. Do call with any questions or comments at all. You can reach me at 1-877-404-3290. That's 1-877-404-3290. It was lovely meeting you and I look forward to our next conversation."*

And with really busy people, email is a great way to agree on a time to have a phone conversation. Your email could say: Hi David, I'm following up on our brief conversation in Toronto last week about my customer service workshops. I look forward to hearing more about your challenges and how I can help. I'm in my office early next week. What time on Monday, Tuesday or Wednesday is best for you in terms of a phone call?

When it comes to leaving messages it is vital to understand that when someone doesn't return your call it's not personal. It's not about you! It's about their hectic life. And not returning your call doesn't mean "no". In fact, if they know the answer is "no", they'll usually call and tell you. But when they're waiting for information from someone else, or the decision has been delayed, or they've been ill...you get the idea. It's not about you.

Finally, in 2013 I made it official—it's no longer rude to not return a call. It certainly used to be and many of us hang on this notion. We judge other people for not getting back to us. So often I hear people say "Well, I can't do anything. I'm waiting for her to call me back." It's definitely time to let this go. If you really want to connect with someone, to build a relationship or move a project forward or confirm a time for a meeting or keep a conversation going, then stop the judgment and take full responsibility for reaching them. After all, you now know how to leave great messages.

The elements I want to include in every message are:

_____

_____

_____

_____

Design one of your well-crafted messages here: ✓

_____

_____

_____

_____

_____

_____

_____

_____

48

Did you know?

For the operators: "Each girl was required to call in every morning at 8:30, having to go to a pay station to do this in most cases, as few had telephones in their own homes. The purpose of this was to ascertain whether, due to someone's possible absence, she would be required at the office for 9 o'clock.

This meant that an operator had to be up and dressed and ready to leave for work even on her mornings off. Some compensation seemed in order, so she was paid 10 cents for the call, whether needed for duty or not."

FROM: The First Century of Service - Bell 1880-1980
Private Printing by Bell, Montreal, 1980, Bell Canada Archives doc. no. 25461

6   *Inspiring Conversation*

We have power in the palms of our hands. We can watch movies, check home security systems, text, play games and answer email. And while all of this is astonishing, our phone's greatest power is its original purpose—connecting us with others in real time, allowing us to hear their voices and engage in conversation.

Of course, as you may have already discovered, it isn't always as simple as dialing a number and speaking. Creating conversation with someone you don't know well—or perhaps don't know at all—takes not only a bit of courage (see Chapter 1), but also some skill.

My failures have taught me these skills. I didn't set out to be a connoisseur of phone communication, but I did set out, at the age of 29, to create a successful business. My lack of sales experience combined with my naiveté about how to talk on the phone created trouble immediately.

One Small Word

I started Media Link Inc., a national research and marketing firm, with a business partner in 1987, and our first task was getting clients. This involved calling organizations across Canada from 8 am every morning, reaching out to the Atlantic coast, to 6 pm each evening connecting to the West.

The results were dismal. While the majority of conversations began well and people were genuinely interested in our innovation and vision, the answer we heard most often was "Certainly send along information but, no thank you."

Rather than accept defeat (although we did start to worry) we decided to focus on our prospects' initial curiosity. How could they be interested in what we were doing yet consistently say "no"? We set up a tape recorder on my phone in order to listen and, hopefully, learn.

And learn we did. My error was evident within the first 10 to 20 seconds of every call, when I said: "This is Mary Jane Copps and I'm just calling..."

The word "just" is a conversation killer. I did use it for good reason. I was 29 years old and calling VPs and CEOs of large organizations so I was nervous. I was holding in my mind's eye that I was interrupting their day. I was striving to be polite. But... what they heard was something completely different.

The word "just" goes across the phone line and says "I'm just calling. I've got nothing better to do. I'm just sitting here dialing numbers." In other words, this call and what I have to say are completely unimportant. And in that moment, (we could hear it happen on the recordings), the other person stopped giving me their full attention.

They are doing the same to you if "just" is part of your phone vocabulary. While they may stay on the call with you for a few moments, they are not really listening and, in most cases, you have lost your ability to inspire conversation.

When I eliminated the word "just" from my phone vocabulary, we started making money—immediately. I have not used it on the phone since 1988.

Two Polite Questions

Speaking on the phone in the late 80's and early 90's was much different than it is today. Voicemail, email, call display and cellphones were not commonplace. Taking calls was something that everyone did. It would have been highly unprofessional not to do so. And there were manners associated with the phone that, if used today, will limit your opportunities to engage in conversation.

The first one is starting a phone call with someone you don't know, or don't know well, with the question "How are you?" While it may sound polite, it actually serves to make the other person defensive. Why? Think about your own reaction to picking up the phone and having a complete stranger say "Hi (your name). How are you today?" What do you think in that moment?

You think the caller is a salesperson, someone who's going to be pushy and is after your money. Our reaction is the result of telemarketing calls we've received over the years, from companies that wanted to us to say "yes" to a cruise, or a computer upgrade, or credit card insurance.

The phrase "How are you?" from someone we don't know or don't know well, makes us suspicious, and it's very difficult to inspire conversation once this happens. It's best to skip the question altogether.

Second is the question "Have I caught you at a good time?" Know that for years and years and years this was an extremely polite question. It was taught as part of every sales program and was regarded as a sign of respect.

This is not the case today.

We have voicemail to answer calls when we are too busy. We have call display to help us determine if we have time to speak to a specific caller. Today, for the most part, we don't answer our phone if we don't have time to speak.

Asking "Have I caught you at a good time?" allows the person you are calling to easily end the call and, obviously, this ends your opportunity to inspire conversation. And for some people, the question even causes annoyance as in "Well, I wouldn't have answered if I didn't have time."

Instead of this question you need to be actively listening each time someone answers your call. There's more about this in the next chapter.

State Your Purpose

No one is sitting in their office or at home waiting for you to call them. Everyone is busy, remember? Every phone call you make is an interruption. You are absolutely reaching them while they are doing something else.

The polite and respectful way to deal with this is...get to the point immediately. For example, *"Hi David, this is Mary Jane calling from The Phone Lady and the reason for my call today is..."*

You can also use "the purpose of my call" or "I'm calling today because" or "this call is about". Use any phrase that lets the person know you are not going to waste their time. You know exactly why you are calling. You have prepared for this call.

If you could watch the person you are calling when you use these phrases, you'd see them stop what they are doing. They might take their hands off their keyboard, or put down their pen, or signal for people to leave their office. They do this because what they hear is respect and this inspires them to give you their full attention...but only for 20 to 30 seconds.

The Pitch

Don't let the word "pitch" make you uncomfortable. It simply means a well-crafted, short and clear description of the reason for your phone call. Today a perfect pitch is brief and precise (ideally 20 seconds, definitely not longer than 30 seconds) and... it inspires conversation.

In those early days of Media Link Inc., when I finally figured out how to structure our phone calls, my pitch was designed to be one minute long—and that was fast at the time. Around the mid-90's, as email began to enter our lives, my pitch had to come in at 30 seconds. Today, with websites enticing us to engage in 20 seconds or less...well, the pressure's on to be quick.

If your reason for calling is related to customer service or administration, then your pitch can be very straightforward. For example:

"Hi David, it's Mary Jane Copps calling from The Phone Lady. The reason for my call today is to verify your attendance at the workshop next week. I'm wondering what information you may need or what questions you have beforehand."

"Hi David, it's Mary Jane Copps calling from The Phone Lady. The reason for my call today is we haven't received a payment for your last invoice. When can we expect that

payment to arrive?"

*"Hi David, it's Mary Jane Copps calling from The Phone
Lady. The reason for my call today is to follow up on last
month's workshop. What has been your team's experience on
the phone since they learned the new skills?"*

If you are calling as part of your sales process, i.e. cold calling
or prospecting, then you need to put effort into crafting your
pitch. It is vital that what you say in your 20 seconds is about
the prospect you are calling, not about you. If you can quickly
present value to a potential client and then ask an open-ended
question, you will inspire a conversation.

For example, I could call a new prospect and say:

*"Hi David, it's Mary Jane Copps calling from The Phone
Lady. The reason for my call today is The Phone Lady has become
a very successful company delivering phone communication
training to businesses throughout North America. I've got a
very impressive client list and offer a wide range of training
options. When are you available to meet with me? "*

The problem with this approach is...it focuses on me, *The
Phone Lady,* and doesn't clearly inform David about the value to
him. If there is value, he's left to figure it out for himself. Chances
are, given how busy he is, he's not going to agree to a meeting. I'll
not only have lost a potential new client but also an opportunity
to build a relationship.

However, if I approach the call this way:

*"Hi David, this is Mary Jane Copps calling from The
Phone Lady. The reason for my call today is I understand you
have a sales team that's responsible for outbound calls to new
customers. The Phone Lady provides workshops on excellent
phone communication, showing sales people how to be more
effective on the phone so they can meet, and exceed, revenue
targets. I'm wondering, what's your process for choosing
training opportunities for your team?"*

This crafted pitch speaks directly to David. It lets him know
I've done my research on his company, which is a sign of respect,

and tells him that my expertise does connect with one of his needs—more revenue.

I end the pitch with an open-ended question. Why? To inspire conversation, to learn more about David and his company, and to discover if there's an opportunity, now or in the future, for us to work together.

Use the template below to craft you own phone pitches. Keep your focus on the person you are calling and end with an open-ended question to get the conversation started:

> *Hi [Their name], this is [Your name] calling from [Your company name]. The reason for my call today is:*

_____

_____

_____

_____

_____

_____

_____

_____

Did you know?

Alexander Graham Bell filed the telephone patent on February 14 1876. Later the same day, Elisha Gray, backed by the telegraph giant Western Union, also filed a caveat (the step before a patent) for a telephone device, though he had not yet built one. Two weeks later, Bell received one of the most valuable patents ever to have been granted— U.S. Patent No. 174,465, dated March 7, 1876 — days after his 29th birthday.

Three days later, he and his assistant, Thomas Watson, succeeded in delivering the first telephonic message: "Mr. Watson, come here, I want to see you."

FROM; Becoming Bell—The Remarkable Story of a Canadian Enterprise by Laurence B. Mussio, PhD
Private Printing by Bell, Montreal, 2005, Bell Canada Archives doc. no. 38013-2

Listen Up!

7

Our ability to listen is what connects us to the "body language" of a phone call. In-person meetings allow us to gather information through eye contact, facial expressions and posture, and sometimes it is our reliance on these cues that make us uncomfortable or fearful on the phone. However, all that information is still there and available to us...through our ears.

And that is the definition of listening—to give attention with the ear. While our ears are hearing constantly throughout each day, we may not be listening. That's why we've all had the experience of someone saying to us "But I already told you that" and yet we have no recollection of the conversation.

Great phone communication demands that we activate our ability to consciously listen—to receive, appreciate and work to understand *everything* that is being expressed in the conversation. This includes taking in not only words, but also tone of voice, background noise and silence.

Conscious listening is what allows us to show respect for clients, customers and potential employers (as well as family and friends), learn from them and build strong relationships.

The first step to activating conscious listening is **eliminating all distraction**. In order to truly hear someone, you can't be doing something else while they are talking (see Chapter 2). Make sure you look away from your computer screen and stop tapping on your keyboard. (*You may have to use the computer as part of delivering customer service. When this is the case, let the other person know that the work you are doing on the computer relates specifically to them*).

Don't drive your car, order coffee or interact with other people when you want to truly listen to someone on the phone.

Pick up a pen. Jotting down key words improves your ability to remember and allows you to record your own thoughts about what you are hearing. This eliminates your need to focus on what you want to say next, as well as your inclination to interrupt. Making quick handwritten notes during a phone conversation is a vital part of conscious listening.

At the beginning of every phone call you want to be consciously listening to the other person's tone of voice as well as sounds in the background. **Reacting to what you hear is a subtle, but important, sign of respect.**

When someone answers their phone you want to **be ready to hear their name**. The beginning of a phone call is the same as shaking someone's hand. Your inattention would be obvious if someone introduced themselves to you and you didn't acknowledge it. Of course, there are people who speak very quickly when they answer the phone, or mumble. In these cases a phrase like *"This is Mary Jane calling from The Phone Lady and I'm sorry, but I didn't catch your name"* will prompt them to clearly repeat it for you.

At the beginning of the call you also want to be **aware of their tone**. Do they answer the phone with stress in their voice? Or distraction? Or are they tremendously rushed? When any of these scenarios occurs, you don't want to ignore what you've heard and continue to focus on your own agenda. To show respect, you must interact with what you hear.

The phrase "It sounds like I've caught you at an inconvenient time" covers most of these situations. It displays respect through its acknowledgement of what you've heard, and allows the other person to choose what happens next. They might say "Yes, I'm running late for a meeting. Can you call me back later today?" or "Sorry, I've been rushing around all morning, but I'm certainly able to speak with you."

And you want to be listening to **background noise** at the beginning of your call. Can you hear lots of people talking? Is the person you are calling driving their car? Are children nearby? Again, you want to acknowledge whatever you hear. In this way it won't remain a distraction throughout the conversation

Statements like *"It sounds like you're in a meeting..."* or *"It sounds like you're driving your car…"* or *"It sounds like the children are home today…"* allow the other person to share with you their specific circumstances. They might respond with "That meeting's just ending. I have time to talk." Or "Yes, I'm in the car but you are on speaker and I have a long drive in front of me, so I have time to talk." Or "Yes, the children are here but they are busy playing on the computer. What can I do for you?"

They may also indicate their preference to have the conversation at another time. Certainly follow their lead and know that, the majority of the time, they will make the effort to take your call because you showed respect.

As outlined in the previous chapter, you begin your conversation by being precise and getting immediately to the point of your call. While you are delivering your "pitch", you are listening for **their reaction**. Do they stay attentive throughout? Or do you hear them get distracted by something or someone else? Do they make any noises, perhaps to interrupt you—like a "uhm" or "but". Or perhaps they sigh, or you hear an "oh" of curiosity?

Listening for these reactions while speaking is something you will develop with practice. And what you hear will allow you to create more powerful conversations.

When someone gets distracted during a 20-to-30 second pitch, your pitch either needs work, you've reached the wrong person, or they are genuinely not interested (at this time) in what you want to share with them.

If someone sighs, it may not mean that they are not interested, but that they receive a lot of similar calls and are making assumptions about where the call is going. This indicates that you need to change course quickly. Ask your open-ended question immediately.

And when someone reacts with curiosity, that's a sign they want to engage. Changing your open-ended question to *"What catches your attention about what I've described?"* is a good way to interact with their curiosity.

Any time you ask a question, **listen consciously to the entire answer**. Don't interrupt. Put aside all of your assumptions. While you may have similar clients, or have heard a similar problem from another customer, the person on the phone with you believes their situation to be unique. In order for you to build or grow a strong relationship, you must hear their story in their own words.

You can help yourself stay focused on what someone is saying by **interacting** with them in small ways. A simple "yes" or "I understand" or "of course", or even an "um hmm", lets them know you are listening and sends a clear signal that you are interested in their story, that you are actively part of the conversation.

Make sure that, while others are talking, your interaction does not cross the line into annoying. For example, the words "right" or "yah" or "okay" can become irritating and are sometimes interpreted as signs that you are bored rather than interested and listening. Take the time to record yourself on the phone occasionally so that you can hear yourself and make adjustments to the words and sounds you choose.

Clarifying what you have heard is a wise practice, particularly in conversations that contain a lot of details, or when your knowledge of the other person's business or circumstance is limited. You can use phrases such as *"Let me share with you what I've heard…"* or *"So what I understand from you is…"* or *"I'd like to review what I've heard to make sure I've understood correctly…"*.

When you clarify you confirm with the other person that you are a conscious listener. You create an opening for the conversation to become more detailed and for the relationship to grow.

Asking **pertinent, open-ended questions** is another way to demonstrate that you have been consciously listening. Based on what you have heard, respond with a question that starts with who, what, when, where, how or why. Or use the very powerful *"Tell me more about… ."*

To learn more about open-ended questions and how to create them, take the time to listen to radio interviews by seasoned journalists. Their ability to create open-ended questions from what has just been said is always a master class in great telephone communication.

At the end of a phone call, **summarize** what you have heard and what will happen next. For example: *"Thank you David, for sharing with me all this information on your customer service team and their phone challenges. What I'll do now is prepare a detailed proposal for you with possible training options. I'll email that to you at the end* *of this week and follow up the next week to address any questions or comments."*

Include the question *"Does this work for you?"* in a summary that includes action items. By asking this question you allow the customer or client to tell you their preferences. Perhaps they want the proposal before the end of the week, to take to a meeting on Thursday night. Or perhaps they are going to be travelling and would prefer that you follow up later in the month.

Remember that asking questions is the best way to get feedback and then hear what the other person is thinking or what they need.

Finally, conscious listening gives you the ability to **understand silence** on the phone. There are many reasons why silence occurs. The other person can be thinking, or taking notes, or distracted, or uninterested, or nervous, or worried, or struggling to find the right words.... .

With practice, you'll "hear" that each type of silence possesses a different quality. You'll be able to tell the difference between an "I'm thinking" silence and an "I'm distracted" silence. These qualities are not something I can put into words, they are experiences of the ear that are available to us when we become conscious listeners.

> *These elements will allow me to display my respect for others and to become a conscious listener:* ✓

1 _____

2 _____

3 _____

4 _____

5 _____

6 _____

7 _____

8 _____

9 _____

10 _____

Did you know?

Eventually, Bell operators became a mainly female force, not only connecting subscribers, but also offering breaking news, the time and the latest hockey scores, tracking down doctors and firefighters when needed; and even offering advice on how to keep the telephone in good working order. Operators soon came to occupy a unique status in the public imagination as remarkable channels of all kinds of information and advice.

FROM; Becoming Bell—The Remarkable Story of a Canadian Enterprise by Laurence B. Mussio, PhD
Private Printing by Bell, Montreal, 2005, Bell Canada Archives doc. no. 38013-2

8 Booking an Appointment

Two things I know to be true: 1) time is our most valuable resource, and 2) meetings take up a lot of our time. So when it comes to booking appointments, it's vital that you approach the task with the utmost respect for time—both a client's and your own.

No matter how efficient we believe ourselves to be, meetings require more time than the spot we give them on our calendar. There's preparing for the meeting, which can range from a few moments to reading a brief email, to an hour for perusing several documents, or even several hours of detailed research.

When the meeting is in your office, you may need a few moments to tidy up, put files away, make room on a desk, table or in a boardroom. Some of you will want to organize tea/coffee/snacks.

When you travel to a meeting, additional time is needed before and after for traffic, parking, elevators, sometimes even getting lost.

Meetings require a minimum of three hours of our time. This is not the case with each individual appointment, but it is a true average of the time it takes to prepare for, travel to, attend and return from a meeting. And then there's the time needed to get refocused on another task.

So before I request or say "yes" to a meeting, I ask myself this question: **Is this in-person meeting absolutely necessary or would another alternative be equally effective?**

There are so many ways for us to "meet". Both video and teleconferencing allow us to not only talk to each other but share documents and computer screens. When appropriate, I offer teleconference training to my clients. Up to 10 people gather around a virtual "table" for one-hour sessions on sales, customer service or job skills. This economical alternative is much appreciated and it saves me a lot of time in airports.

But some circumstances call for getting together in person. Information may be sensitive, confidential and a private meeting is the best way to share all the details. There could be a creative element to the work you are doing and brainstorming together will produce better results. And sometimes miscommunication has taken place that can best be resolved face to face.

When a face-to-face meeting is the best choice, then I answer this question: **What is the most efficient way to get agreement on a date and time for the meeting?**

Many of us have come to rely on email and text messaging for booking appointments and often, if our client or prospect does a lot of business travel, this is the best way to communicate across time zones. And email has the ability to link directly with personal calendars, adding another appreciated, and often expected, level of efficiency. But ...

Email can also produce both irritation and frustration, especially when it comes to agreeing on when and where to meet. We have all been part of a seemingly endless stream of messages that contain phrases like: "That date's good for me, but only after 3 pm." "Can't do it after 3, so how about the following Friday?" "Travelling Friday but can do the following Tuesday." And on and on and on. This is disrespectful of everyone's time and a clear indication that a phone call will be more efficient.

In the phone call you want to use very specific language. Here's the why and how:

I receive calls or emails almost every day from someone who would like to meet with me. And I'm honoured that they are interested in me and *The Phone Lady*, and want to share their time. Usually the request is for coffee, which sounds quick and efficient, but after many (many) years of coffee meetings, I know better.

As soon as the question is asked, I look up at my four-month schedule that fills one wall of my office. Almost every block has something in it—a workshop, a coaching session, a board meeting, scheduled prospecting, planning and writing time. The few white spaces remaining are often needed for projects that go into overtime, or for writing proposals, or to spend time with family and friends.

When I look at that schedule, especially when I'm on the phone and someone's waiting for an answer, I get completely overwhelmed and tongue-tied. I start sputtering and muttering because what I'm looking at tells me that I have time for coffee... in four or five months.

Of course, that doesn't make any sense, but in that moment on the phone that's what I see. Now, I don't say that; it would sound both crazy and rude. What I do say is "Let me confirm a few things on my schedule and I'll get back to you with some possibilities."

Sound familiar? I'm guessing that many of you, especially those in sales, are hearing something similar a lot of the time.

As I've mentioned before (and likely will again), everyone is overwhelmed. We all have too much to do and often confirming the where and when of another meeting is simply too much to deal with quickly. Instead we offer a "maybe".

And "maybe" is a whole lot more work for everyone. Still using the example above, I would end the call and, with any luck, make a decision right away about options for the meeting, then send a short email. A prompt reply and coffee would be confirmed in our calendars within hours.

But that's the ideal and rare. In all likelihood as soon as I hang up from that call, I'll get distracted by something else, or re-engaged in what I was doing prior to the call, and perhaps forget to look for suitable times to meet. Or, given my hectic schedule, simply procrastinate on making a decision. If the other person doesn't follow up (more on this in the next chapter) then the meeting may be lost forever.

The caller is left waiting for meeting options from me and wondering how to follow up if I don't get back to them. Should they call me in a few days? A week? My inability to book the meeting in one phone call has left them with more decisions to make about their own time and schedule.

So...what to do?

Well, if you have determined that a meeting is indeed necessary you must help the person make a decision about time and place while you are both on the phone. Make it your responsibility to inspire a decision in one call. This is respectful of everyone's time.

Here's how you do it—instead of asking something like "When is it convenient for you to meet with me for a quick coffee?" or "What does your schedule look like in terms of our getting together?", which leads to the overwhelmed-and-unable-to-give-an-answer scenario, be very specific.

Say something like *"What does your schedule look like next week, say Tuesday or Thursday afternoon, to get together for coffee?"* or *"I'm going to be near your office next week, on Wednesday morning and Friday afternoon. Will either of those times work for you?"*

Going back once more to my example, if you were to call me and use one of these statements, instead of looking at my full four-month crazy schedule, I'd focus only on the days mentioned. I may indeed find a time slot for coffee, but if I don't, my eyes naturally travel to the following week and it is easier for me to suggest alternative dates and times.

While there are certainly situations when travel and work schedules make meetings very difficult to organize, this technique of being specific, which I use on behalf of myself and my clients, achieves success. Practice it and rely on it. You will increase your appointment bookings.

Before booking a meeting, ask yourself these two questions:

First...

"Is this in-person meeting absolutely necessary or would another alternative be equally effective?"

Second...

"What is the most efficient way to get agreement on a date and time for the meeting?"

Did you know?

On another occasion, my partner and I were running a jumper wire in the New London telephone office. The door opened and in walked an elderly gentleman. This man asked my partner if he would pull a tooth for him. My partner was too nervous so he asked me to pull the tooth. I didn't want to but I could see the old fellow was suffering. Finally, I took out my six inch pliers and pulled the tooth in one fast motion. The relief shone on his face and he thanked me and walked out the door.

Submitted by Richard F. Jeffery

FROM: Telephone Stories by Telephone People, Edited by A. Gordon Archibald

71

Persistence = Success

9

Persistence is already part of your life. Since you were a child you've been using it to learn new skills and get things done.

One of my first memories of being persistent relates to whistling. My brother, older by five years, was a great whistler and he teased me mercilessly because when I tried to create sound, nothing happened. So what did I do? I practiced and practiced and practiced. I'd keep family members waiting for the bathroom while I stood in front of the mirror blowing air until one day…music came out.

Persistence is also how I learned to ride a bike, multiply, bake, write and…create successful businesses. Richard DeVos, co-founder of Amway, says "If I had to select one quality, one personal characteristic that I regard as being most highly correlated with success, whatever the field, I would pick the trait of persistence."

Yet, when I stand in front of a room of people and talk to them about persistence and follow up, almost everyone gets uncomfortable. "But I don't want to be a pest," someone will say, while everyone around them nods in agreement.

There is a big difference between professional follow up and being a pest.

You are a pest when you:

• Continue to call people who can't benefit from your product or service;
• Don't accept "no" as a valid decision;

• Are only interested in money, not a relationship;

• Continue to push your agenda without listening to the prospect/employer;

and I'm sure there's more, but you get the idea.

You are being persistent when you approach those you know can benefit from what you are offering and take responsibility for creating clear and professional communication.

Persistence is defined as being constant and comes from the Latin *constare* which means to stand firm, stay resolute and faithful. When you follow up with your clients, prospects, employment possibilities, you prove (each time) that you are confident in what you have to offer and that you value the relationship. Your actions say that you are steadfast and can be trusted. And trust is the essential building block of all relationships.

In business there are three key points where persistence and follow up are essential.

1 When you want to create a new relationship.

On the phone you begin to establish trust the moment you leave your first message. This is when you extend your hand in introduction and create your first impression (see Chapter 5).

These messages need to be precise. It's also important that you take full responsibility for establishing contact. Creating and playing "phone tag" results in unnecessary frustration and…it's rude.

Here's a message that works when reaching out to someone you do not know:

"Hi David Potter. This is Mary Jane Copps calling from The Phone Lady. I have a quick question for you and I'm in my office today until 3 pm. You can reach me at 902-404-3290. That's 902-404-3290. If we don't connect by 3 pm today, know that I'll follow up with you again on Friday."

The key elements of this message are: a) the word "quick" helps them decide to return the call, even if they only have five minutes between meetings (Of course, be sure you truly have only one quick question.); b) it is not filled with lots of detail, which can cause frustration for the listener and influence them to say "no" to the message, destroying any opportunity of having a conversation; c) it states your availability, therefore eliminating phone tag; d) the phone number is left clearly, twice; and e) it lets the contact know that you'll keep trying to reach them. This indicates that you believe your call to be of value and, since you're going to keep calling, it often influences the contact to return your call.

So what happens then, if you leave a message only once or perhaps twice and then stop? What impression do you create? Well, visualize extending your hand to introduce yourself to someone and then…withdrawing it.

When you leave messages for someone and then stop, you are still saying something: I've decided I don't want to work with you; my product really isn't valuable to you; I'm unorganized; I've lost your number ; it's all about making a fast sale so I've moved on.

Experience has taught me that, in business-to-business communication, leaving five messages is the best performance standard. Why? Well, when I call someone I don't' know, they listen to my first and second messages and often think "Hmm, Mary Jane Copps. I don't know her. If it's important she'll call back." On messages three and four, they do write down to call me back but then their day gets hectic and this task doesn't make the priority list.

Know that not every new contact will require five messages from you, especially if your messages are precise and you take full responsibility for connecting. What's key is that you don't give up. After five messages, if you really want to stop, you can leave a message like this:

"Hi David Potter. It's Mary Jane Copps calling from The Phone Lady. Sorry I've missed you. I do want to connect at your convenience and I welcome hearing from you. You can reach me at 902-404-3290. That's 902-404-3290. Thanks so much."

How often should you call? It depends on what you want to

accomplish. If you are in advertising sales and have a deadline, calling once every two days is certainly acceptable. When there's no impending deadline, leave a message at least once a week. Leaving two or three weeks between messages infers that the call is unimportant.

2 When you have presented information to a client or employer for their review.

Our ability to follow up on conversations, presentations and/or material creates our reputation for excellence. And yet the majority of people give up way too soon. Making this follow up happen is crucial to success.

Here's a sample follow up message:

> *"Hi David, it's Mary Jane, The Phone Lady, calling to hear your questions and comments on my recent proposal. I'm in my office throughout the day today and can be reached at 902-404-3290. That's 902-404-3290. If we don't connect today, I'll follow up with you later this week. Thanks."*

The message remains precise; it does not create phone tag.

Where things get complicated is when the message is not returned. You are going to be tempted to take it personally because you've presented information, you've showed them who you are, perhaps demonstrated your product/service. The lack of response suddenly feels personal.

You need to…get over it! It's not personal, it's not emotional—it's business.

Your prospect or prospective employer is considering the value you bring to their company. They are not making a decision about you on a personal level. Don't allow your ego to get in the way of faithful follow up.

Here are a few of the reasons prospects/employers don't return follow up calls:

- They have not reviewed your information thoroughly and at the moment don't have any questions or comments;

- They have shared the information with others on their team and are waiting for that feedback;

- Their company has landed a huge new contract and everyone's full attention is needed at the moment;

- They are ill or there is another important personal reason that has kept them away from the office;

- They are travelling and having difficulty keeping up with messages.

Here's what I know to be true. When someone doesn't call back after meeting with you and/or accepting your information, it rarely, if ever, means "no". When it is definitely no, they will tell you. But when they have no news, when they have yet to organize their questions or when their lives are beyond hectic, they may not be able to call you back. You demonstrate your belief in the relationship and you prove you are trustworthy by continuing to follow up.

Of course, many of you are following up by email. You write a quick note—something like: "Following up on my proposal. Look forward to your questions and comments." And then you wait—and wait—and wait.

Sending a follow up message by email is completely professional. Waiting for a response for days or weeks...or months, is unprofessional.

Email is not a "sure thing". It often arrives in an overflowing inbox. It can be sent to spam. It can be filed in the wrong folder. It can simply be missed in the day-to-day deluge of communication. Don't sit in the silence and wait; pick up the phone. (See Chapter 11 for more information on the relationship between email and phone communication.)

3 When you have completed work for a client.

Most of us do not make time for this important and valuable

aspect of communication (myself included). When everything's done and the client says "thanks", we get caught up in the next set of proposals, presentations, etc.

Shame on us!

When you finish a project with a client, follow up to hear their feedback. And follow up in one month, or six months, to hear how things are going. These calls are not about selling, (although more work is often the result), they are about building stronger relationships and creating an opportunity for you to grow and learn.

It doesn't matter if you are a sales person, entrepreneur, job seeker or customer service representative, following up after you work with a client is the best way to learn how to improve.

At this stage, the follow up does not have to be, in fact shouldn't be, a series of messages. It can be one phone message such as:

> *"Hi David, it's Mary Jane calling. I really enjoyed spending the day with your team. It was a lot of fun. I do want to hear your feedback so contact me at your convenience at 902-404-3290. That's 902-404-3290. I look forward to our next conversation."*

This message can be followed up by an email and there's great value in including the client in your regular marketing efforts. Whether it's a blog, newsletter, social media or a combination of all these, create a way to stay in touch so that the client continually experiences how much you value the relationship.

Remember, being constant in your follow up proves you are trustworthy. Put your discomfort aside and pick up the phone!

Follow Up Requires Organization

One of the main reasons people falter when it comes to follow up is they haven't got the right system in place to stay organized. It is crucial to success that you do not misplace names and phone numbers, that you call when you say you're going to call, that you keep your word.

The system I most often encounter when working with clients

is...the spreadsheet and I have to say it is not a good follow up system. It's difficult to maintain accurate notes, it does not remind you when you need to make a call, it does not store email correspondence or proposals. Perhaps, if you only have 10 to 20 people on your follow up list, and commit to looking at your spreadsheet every day, it might work, but as a rule, it has too much room for error and does not allow for all of the important details.

There's entering the contact's name into your calendar each time you want to call them. While this works, it still does not give you access to all the information you need.

Persistence and follow up success are directly related to having a customer relationship management (CRM) system in place. There are hundreds of options to choose from today, so take the time to find one that suits your needs and your vision for growth. I've used an online system called *Highrise* for several years and am very pleased with both its simplicity and its detail. I can look at a client or prospect file and access everything I need—contact information, history, correspondence, proposals—everything.

So, your assignment for this chapter? Investigate a wide variety of CRMs and choose one that fits your needs and price point.

Did you know?

I remember one night around midnight two men came to the door. At this time the booth was inside the office. They...were very drunk, and they wanted to put a call through to their homes. In no way was I going to open that door! I told them I'd put their messages through and after a lot of swearing and argument they consented but I wasn't to make it a collect call.

After the message went through they then insisted on coming in to pay for the call which amounted to thirty-five cents. I refused to open the door and after a bit more snarling and thumping around they left. In the morning, when I opened the door there was thirty-five cents on the doorstep.
Submitted by Margaret Ruth Bagnell

FROM: Telephone Stories by Telephone People, Edited by A. Gordon Archibald

Review Notes

Reaching the Right Person

10

Connecting with the right person can be intimidating; it's one of the major reasons people avoid the phone. There are tips and tricks for almost every situation, which is the focus of this chapter, but there's work to be done even before you dial.

In the late '80s, one of the first employees my business partner and I hired for Media Link Inc., was a researcher. Their job was to read newspapers and magazines, listen to the radio and watch television news programs and find me, the salesperson, the right people to call. Everyday my inbox would fill up with highlighted clippings and handwritten notes with names and titles of individuals recently mentioned or interviewed in the media. These were my best leads. It was worth a full-time salary to have the right name prior to my placing a call.

That's still the case today but…all the necessary research is at your fingertips, no highlighter or scissors necessary.

The best place to start is a **corporate website** which often offers a "Meet the Team" or "Executive Profiles" page, where you can easily find the names and titles of much of the staff or, at the very least, the main executives for each division. If this isn't available, you can search the website using a key word that relates to your area of interest, i.e. marketing, human resources, engineering, etc., and names may appear on press releases or blog entries.

If this doesn't give you anything of value, head to *LinkedIn* where a search by company name will usually deliver the name and title of the right individual. If this still doesn't give you what you need, enter the company name and title into your **search engine**. For example, "ABC Company VP Marketing". The name may appear in relation to volunteer work they do, awards they've won or associations of which they are a member.

In doing this research, you may be lucky enough to come across your contact's direct phone number, then all you'll need to do is leave great messages and stay persistent (see Chapters 5 and 9).

But when you don't have a direct line you will either end up speaking to a receptionist and/or executive assistant, or using an automated phone directory. When you have the name of the person you want to reach, an **automated system** does not pose much of a challenge. Most of the time, you simply need to start spelling the person's first or last name when prompted. If you do encounter difficulties or if spelling on a phone key pad is difficult for you (as is the case with many, many people), you can usually choose "0" and reach a receptionist.

Connecting with a **receptionist** is, for many people, the most intimidating part of phone communication. But understanding and working with receptionists is a vital part of the process. As with everything else in this book, you will get better with a bit of knowledge and some practice.

Receptionists have a job to do and it's your respect for this job that allows you to reach the right person. Receptionists are responsible for the efficiency of their company's incoming phone communication. This includes identifying calls that might be "unnecessary", i.e. sales calls, calls that they can handle themselves or send to a different department, etc. As soon as they answer the phone, they are using all of their listening skills in order to determine the best way to handle the call.

As part of displaying your respect, you want to be present and using all your listening skills (see Chapter 7) as soon as the receptionist answers the phone. Many will include their names as part of their greeting and you want to hear and use it during your conversation. You want to honour the handshake they are extending, for example:

Receptionist: *ABC Company, Natasha speaking. How can I help you?*

Me: Hi *Natasha. It's Mary Jane calling from The Phone*

Lady. Is David available?

Because they are charged with keeping out unnecessary calls, calls that make the company less efficient (hence the term "gatekeeper"), receptionists are constantly on guard for people who are too pushy or too charming. By using the receptionist's name and introducing yourself, you include them in your communication with the company—you show respect—and alleviate suspicion.

It is also valuable to remain informal when asking for your chosen contact. I learned this trick as a journalist. When I called to connect with sources for interviews, there was always a deadline looming. Explaining the full reason for my call, the magazine or newspaper I was calling from, etc., often slowed me down and increased my stress level. So, whether I knew the person I was calling or not, I would simply ask for them by first name.

When you do this, the receptionist is less likely to ask you additional questions. What they "hear" is that you are a known business associate, a close friend, a family member, a lover, etc. Most of the time, they will put you through to the person you've requested.

But sometimes they do ask a few questions. You should always be prepared for this to happen and confident in your answers.

The questions asked by receptionists (the "gatekeepers") are the very foundation of phone fear. People believe this is the moment they will stumble and make a fool of themselves and ruin any opportunity to ever reach the right person. This doesn't have to be the case because…here are the most common questions:

1 *"What is the company name?"* or *"What company are you calling from please?"*

There's no reason to be uncomfortable when you answer this question. Simply state your company name and do it with confidence, i.e. *"I'm calling from The Phone Lady."*

2 *"What is the reason for your call?"* The answer here needs to be precise, efficient. Do not start giving the receptionist your well-crafted pitch. That's not efficient. My preference is to say *"I'm calling in regards to an upcoming sales workshop"* or *"It's in regards to customer service training"*. Again, whatever the reason for your call, say it with confidence. If you provide an answer but sound unsure of yourself, you will inspire more questions.

3 *"Is so-and-so expecting your call?"* The best answer to this question is always the truth. When I'm prospecting people I've never spoken to before I'll either answer with only "no" or with one of these options: *"No, not today." "No, I don't believe so." "No, we haven't connected yet."*

Remember if you answer "yes" and it's not true, there is every possibility you will get caught in that lie and definitely ruin any possibility of connecting with the right person.

4 *"Is there someone else who can help you?"* My answer to this, because I've done my research and know I have the correct contact name, is always *"No, I don't believe so, but thank you for asking."*

Sometimes, no matter how much research you do, you simply can't find the name and phone number of the person you want to reach. This is when you want to **engage the power of the word "help"**. For example:

"ABC Company. Natasha speaking."

"Hi Natasha. This is Mary Jane calling from The Phone Lady. I'm wondering if you can help me."

"I'll try."

"I'm trying to locate the name of your current customer service manager. Who would that be?"

"Oh, that's Jay Helmer."

"Thanks. Is he available?"

The word "help" dissolves almost all defences. Most people like to be helpful. So instead of sparking suspicion, you are able to work with the receptionist and identify your contact very quickly.

It's very important to ask for the name first, prior to asking to be put through. Otherwise, you may reach an extension without a name, or where the name is unclear, and you'll have to go through the whole process with the receptionist a second time.

Now, it's possible for companies to not have a receptionist, or for a receptionist to be unhelpful. What to do then? Here are three choices that I have used for years with great success:

- If the company is publicly traded, full contact information for the **Investor Relations** person will be easily available on the website. This person is responsible for communicating with current and potential investors and, as a consequence, is usually lovely. Call them on their direct line and say:

"Sorry to trouble you. I'm looking for the name of your current VP of Marketing. Would you have that information?"

Or

"I'm wondering if you can help me. I'm wanting to connect with your current VP of Marketing. Can you provide me with their name and number?"

- Many companies also have press releases available at their website and at the bottom of most press releases is the contact information for a **Media or Public Relations** person. You can use the same approach as with Investor Relations. Do make sure the media relations person works at the company you are researching. Some companies hire external professionals for this job and contacting them will not be productive.

- Go to the top—the **Executive Assistant (EA) of the CEO**. Years ago I did a project for a local client, *NovaScotian Crystal*. They are North America's only mouth-blown, hand-cut crystal maker, and they were expanding into a new market. Their artisan products are commissioned for trophies, holiday and retirement gifts, and awards. I was at a complete loss when it came to identifying whom I should speak to within a company. I didn't think that asking a receptionist to be connected to the person who buys crystal would work. So, for every call, I asked to be connected to the EA of the CEO.

This strategy works for a number of reasons: a) the receptionist views the EA of the CEO as a colleague, not a superior, so rarely asks additional questions. Most often, you will be put through directly; b) the EA of the CEO is the public face and voice of the CEO so the majority of the time she (and they are usually a "she") is lovely; c) she knows everyone in the company and their responsibilities, so you can count on being connected to the right person; and d) when you call that person and say *"I've been directed to you by the CEO's office,"* you receive their full attention.

The whole process of reaching the right person is much easier when you have a **referral**. This is the joy of social networks like *LinkedIn*, where you can request introductions through your 1st and 2nd level connections.

When you can call a receptionist and say *"Hi Natasha, it's Mary Jane Copps calling for Jay Helmer. I've been referred to him by David Potter"* everything works very smoothly.

And when you leave a message for Jay Helmer, or reach him for a conversation, you can start the conversation with *"The reason for my call today is I've been referred to you by… . "*

I've been calling people I don't know for over 27 years and at least 33% of the time, I haven't had a name or phone number. How many times have I not reached the right person? About a dozen—out of thousands and thousands of calls. The strategies above work. Have confidence and practice.

Be ready for the diligent receptionist and prepare your answers to these common questions:

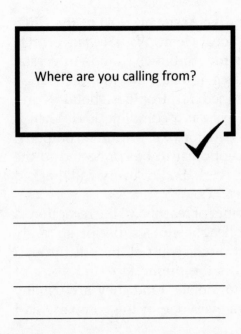

Where are you calling from?

What is the reason for your call?

✓

_____

_____

_____

_____

Is she/he expecting your call?

✓

_____

_____

_____

_____

_____

Did you know?

By March of 1880 the newly organized Bell Telephone Company was in control of 60,000 American telephones. Improvements in switchboard technology allowed operators to handle not tens of calls, but hundreds. The first operators were boys who earned a reputation for being rude and abusive. The necessity of running from one board to another made for chaos in the telephone exchanges. The young men were soon traded for young women who did not swear or trade insults with frustrated customers, and were said to be faster than the men they replaced. American women, until then largely consigned to the schoolhouse and home took over the day-to-day management of the switchboards. These women worked 12-hour shifts processing hundreds of calls each hour working the board with both hands at once. They were expected to follow a strict code of dress and behavior. The company actually kept a deportment card to record transgressions. The operator was not allowed to cross her legs. She was forbidden to blow her nose or wipe her brow without permission. Those who married were often discharged. Nevertheless, by 1910 New York Telephone alone had over 6,000 women working at switchboards.

FROM: Use of Women as Telephone Operators, video created by the Museum of Independent Telephony, Dickinson County Historical Society, Dickinson County Heritage Center, Abilene, Kansas, USA

Review Notes

Phone vs Email

It's important that I start off this chapter by saying "I'm not anti-email".

My first 14 years as an entrepreneur involved a lot of direct mail. Usually we'd send out new information or special offers to prospects twice each year. The design and execution of these campaigns was incredibly time consuming.

The process included:

1   Identifying the prospects i.e. going through thousands of index cards;

2   Confirming, by phone, that we had the correct postal address and contact name;

3   Designing and printing a campaign-specific brochure that would attract attention;

4   Writing a letter to go with the brochure;

5   Stuffing and sealing envelopes;

6   Paying for the necessary postage, going to the post office; and

7   Waiting up to 10 days to follow up.

I always enjoyed creating the new brochure but the rest of it, especially the days of waiting between the mailing and the follow up call, made me crazy. So when email arrived in my life, I was thrilled.

And I still am. It remains amazing to me that I can speak to someone on the phone and within minutes deliver to them a summary of our conversation, marketing material or a proposal. Email allows me—and you - to seize the moment.

But email has its weaknesses. In order to communicate effectively, you need to understand and avoid them. If you don't, you stand to lose a client, a prospect or a friend.

Black and White

The first thing to acknowledge about email is—it's a black and white medium. It exists to transfer information and data, i.e. facts, between two points, quickly. It does not have the ability to listen, understand or clarify. Everything else is either implied by the writer or the reader. And that's where the things can get… messy.

Here's one of my favorite examples:

A print advertising salesperson I was coaching was struggling to reach his target. When we crunched the numbers we forecast he would be short about $5,000. In discussions with the editor and publisher, we came up with an idea for one of the publication's most loyal advertisers. It would not only create the necessary funds to reach budget, but also provide great value for this client.

The salesperson quickly sent off an email describing the opportunity, its impact and the pricing structure. The response he received was "Yeah, we might be interested in that."

Upon reading that response my advice was to call the client. It was not clear to me what the client was saying. But the salesperson knew this client, had met him several times, they had attended events and dinners together, so his reaction was "No, this is good. He's going to do it."

In fact, the salesperson was so confident that the client was going to go ahead with the proposal, he relaxed, stopped pushing himself to uncover new possibilities.

When the day arrived to close out the issue, there was still no confirmation that the client was going ahead with the $5,000 advertising package. A phone call was made and, much to everyone's disappointment, the final answer was a resounding "no". The magazine closed below budget.

The lesson?

When we read email, we "hear" or imply a tone of voice.

When the email is from someone we know really, really well, the tone we choose to apply to the words is often correct. But for emails from colleagues, clients or co-workers…we can completely misinterpret what's being said.

When the salesperson read "Yeah, we might be interested in that", he heard a very energetic "yeah" followed by an enthusiastic "we might be interested in that". It's what he wanted to hear. It didn't even occur to him that the statement could be said casually and with very little interest.

However, if he'd picked up the phone to follow up on that email… .

Peter F. Drucker, the renowned management consultant, educator and author said: "The most important thing in communication is to hear what isn't being said." This is what the phone allows us to do.

Phone conversations are powerful because we can hear what someone is thinking. Their thoughts are contained not only in the words they choose, but in how they say those words. We can respond to those thoughts, in the moment, creating opportunities that often evaporate in the time and space between emails.

If the salesperson had called the client and heard the lack of enthusiasm for the proposal, he could have asked *What would make this work for you?* or *How can we make this work for you?* There may have been another opportunity, another way, to work together. We'll never know.

The telephone delivers moments of conversation, the back and forth of questions and answers, the sharing of thoughts and feelings. And this is how relationships are built. Whether you are involved in a job search, sales, customer service or accounts receivable, building relationships is your goal. Relationships are what make both careers and companies prosper.

Overlooked or Lost

Email is also impacted by "overwhelm" — that constant state of rush that has become part of our daily lives. As *The Phone Lady*, I receive upwards of 250 emails a day. (Once in a while I close my eyes and try to imagine what this would look like if it were delivered to me by regular post. Yikes!)

We have all embraced the illusion that every time we click "send", we've communicated, but that's not always the case.

It is brash, perhaps arrogant, of us to assume that all of the email we send is received, read and considered. There is so much email that messages do get "buried" in inboxes, are misfiled and often lost in spam folders.

On the other hand, when we speak with someone on the phone, we know the conversation has taken place. No guesswork, no assumptions — only communication.

When You Say "Hmmmm"

Clear communication is the responsibility of both the speaker/writer and the listener/reader. When you are reading email messages, if at any time you say "Hmmm, I wonder what they meant by that?", respect that voice of doubt. Pick up the phone and get some clarity before spending the time creating an ineffective response to the wrong question.

Time Consuming

Email can cause tremendous delays when it comes to decision making. The most common example of this is reaching agreement on a date and time. You send a message suggesting 1 pm on Tuesday. The other person answers saying that doesn't work for them, how about Wednesday morning at 10 am. You respond by saying that you have meetings all day Wednesday. What about Friday? And this can go on and on and on.

When we speak to each other on the phone we can navigate the decision-making process together. Whether it's about choosing a date and time or launching a new product, an outcome can be reached.

Pairing Phone Calls and Email

You can be more efficient and create clear and concise communication by combining phone calls and email.

For example:

I worked with a client creating an annual directory for seniors for several years. About 100 individuals, companies and organizations advertised in this directory and my job was to contact them and verify they wanted to participate for another year.

The first step of the process was a phone call and I was quite content if I reached voicemail. My message was *"Hi, it's Mary Jane calling because I'm working on the upcoming issue of ABC publication and I want to confirm that you'll be participating again this year. I'm going to take the liberty of sending you all the information by email today. You can reply with your confirmation and, if I don't hear from you, I'll follow up with you again in two weeks."*

This combination of phone call and email substantially increased the chances that the email message was received, read and considered. In fact, this approach always brought in my first burst of revenue on this project.

Whenever you send out a resume, invitation, brochure, statement or invoice to someone who is not anticipating or expecting it, consider combining that email with a phone call. You will definitely improve your outcomes.

Another way to combine phone and email relates to working with our rapidly changing technology. The number of business executives, and businesses, that now rely solely on cellphones for communication is steadily increasing. While I don't anticipate the total disappearance of business landlines any time soon, I'm closely following trends and learning new skills every time I make prospecting calls.

Cellphones can make it more difficult to reach decision makers for impromptu discussions and conversations. Email is the ideal way to set a date and time for a phone call. We are definitely headed in the direction of phone calls needing to be scheduled, similar to meetings. While this is already creating difficult communication challenges when it comes to prospecting, it's also supporting a renewed interest in productive, focused phone calls.

Short and Simple

When email first arrived in our lives, we treated it like our existing tactile methods of communication. We started messages with "Dear So and So," and we aimed for perfect grammar and paragraph structure. We brought to the task the skills we had been using to write letters or memos on 8 1/2 by 11 inch paper.

In these early days I remember staff coming to me when they received a short, one-line answer from a client or prospect. The short blast of information made them feel uncomfortable and they assumed it was written in anger or frustration.

But these early adopters of few words are actually my champions of email. While good grammar and spelling remain vital, truly effective email is short and to the point. You want to deliver information without the necessity of scrolling down.

Leave white space between thoughts and ideas. This increases both the speed at which the information can be read and the reader's ability to retain that information.

Use numbers or symbols to separate specific points or thoughts. This also supports clarity, speed and retention.

And proofread what you've written, several times—and at least once out loud. Reading out loud helps you discover what your reader will "hear" and helps you eliminate potential confusion.

Effective communication occurs when we: say exactly what we mean and not more; don't take anything for granted; put aside our assumptions; and are forthright about what we don't understand. Read and write your email with this in mind and, when in doubt, pick up the phone.

Did you know?

Prior to 1973, mobile telephony was limited to phones installed in cars and other vehicles. Motorola was the first company to produce a handheld mobile phone. On 3 April 1973 when Martin Cooper, a Motorola researcher and executive, made the first mobile telephone call from handheld subscriber equipment, placing a call to Dr. Joel S. Engel of Bell Labs, the prototype handheld phone used by Dr. Cooper weighed 1.1 kg and measured 23 cm long, 13 cm deep and 4.45 cm wide. The prototype offered a talk time of just 30 minutes and took 10 hours to re-charge.

From:
https://en.wikipedia.org/wiki/Martin_Cooper_(inventor)

What's Best

Developing business and building relationships:
1st Your tone of voice will inspire curiosity; your ability to listen will create opportunity
2nd Follow up by email to communicate details.

You want to make a complaint:
1st Your voice will clearly communicate the need for immediate action
2nd Follow up by email to communicate details and confirm agreement.

Phone

An immediate decision is necessary:
1st Reaching someone on the phone is the fastest way to confirm or gather information
2nd Follow up by email to have a record of agreement.

Uncertainty or conflict exists:
1st Tone can be implied in an email; call to confirm what you think is being said or resolve conflict
2nd Follow up by email to confirm understanding and record details.

When...

You want to communicate detailed information:

1st Organize information in an email so it's easy to understand and refer back to.

2nd Follow up by phone to confirm receipt and understanding.

You need to reach a lot of people fast:

1st Use a bulk email application to reach hundreds of people in minutes.

2nd Follow up by phone when readers show interest by clicking.

eMail

Working with others on projects:

1st Use emails to document action items, deadlines, milestones, decisions, meeting minutes, etc.

2nd Follow up by phone to enforce accountability.

Care and forethought are necessary:

1st An email may be edited many times before being sent to ensure the message is exactly right.

2nd You'll feel more confident about the follow-up phone call.

Difficult Conversations

Each of us have tasks and challenges we find difficult, but when it comes to phone communication there are several situations everyone struggles with from time to time. These conversations require extra effort and skill in order for everyone to be heard and understood. Let's take a look at two of them:

The Upset Customer

This is the most common difficult conversation in business and the one I'm asked about in every workshop. The key to communicating with someone who's upset is empathy— understanding what they are feeling and how this impacts them.

The majority of the time, the strategies below result in improved communication and a more satisfied customer. They work best when you remain calm, take nothing personally and give your full attention to both what the customer says and how they say it.

1 **Emotion vs Logic:** When someone calls to complain they are emotional—upset, angry, disappointed, frustrated— or perhaps all of these. Their right brain is fully in control and the rational, logical and sequential abilities of the left brain are simply not available to them. (Interestingly enough, the left brain controls our verbal abilities as well.) They are unable to participate in logical conversation. The best way to fully understand this is to think about your own life and someone very close to you. Remember the last time you had a conversation with this person during which both of you were emotional. Now, which one of you was listening? The answer is—neither of you—because when our right brain is fully in charge, we cannot hear and cannot logically process information.

So there is absolutely no value trying to engage an upset customer in a logical conversation until they have finished telling you the story of why they are upset. I realize this can occasionally make for a very long phone call, but...they are the customer so you need to allow them this time. Given their emotional state, interrupting them is equivalent to throwing fuel on a fire. It will increase their level of distress and make your ability to resolve the situation much more difficult.

2 **Speed:** Upset customers often speak very quickly and, as a consequence, are difficult to hear and understand. This doesn't help you solve their problem. So use the phone's ability to act like a mirror. Talk more slowly and maintain a calm and pleasant tone of voice. The customer will soon follow your lead and although this won't solve their problem, it will improve your ability to understand them.

3 **Apologize:** I get a lot of pushback on this suggestion, but it has never failed me—apologize near the beginning of the conversation. Once the customer has told you their story, given you every detail about why they are upset, the first words out of your mouth should be "I'm sorry". I'm not advocating that you take the blame for anything, but know that the customer wants an apology. The sooner they hear it, the sooner you can move on to solving the problem. You can say something like: *"I'm so sorry, we never want any of our customers to feel this way"* or *"I'm sorry, this is not something we want any of our customers to experience"*. Your customer needs to know that they are important to you and that you empathize with their situation. An apology does all of that. It calms them down, makes them slightly less defensive; it improves your ability to communicate with them.

4 **Ignite Their Left Brain:** In order to resolve the situation, you must inspire your customer to talk *with* you, not *at* you. They need to be able to listen to you, respond to questions, provide more information, etc. So you need to help them get out of that place of pure emotion (right brain) and into a place of logic and sequential thinking (left brain). You do this by asking them an open-ended question, a question they will have to think about in order to answer. Once they start thinking, they will connect with their left brain and you'll be able to start working towards a resolution.

You don't want to make any promises. This is simply about creating a productive conversation where both sides can hear each other and share information. Here are some examples: *"I'm so sorry, David. We don't want any of our customers to find themselves in this situation. Tell me, what are you hoping will happen next?"* or *"I'm so sorry, David. We never want any of our customers to feel this way. What other details can you give me that will help us find a solution?"*

5 **Put Your Ego Away:** Dealing with an upset customer is never about who's right and who's wrong—it's about creating a positive experience and discovering the facts of the situation. Do not allow your need to be right enter into the conversation. This creates animosity, defensiveness and miscommunication.

6 **Pick Up The Phone:** Under no circumstances should you use email to communicate with an upset customer. You need to hear their tone of voice and engage them in conversation in order to be sure you've uncovered all the information and satisfied their concerns. When the customer is happy with how their complaint is handled they not only remain your customer, but they share their experience with others. Every upset customer offers us a chance to grow our business.

The Constant Talker

This person loves a good, long conversation and believes the stories they have to tell are vital and necessary. In fact, their stories are so vital and necessary they are often worth repeating again—and again—and again.

Being on the phone with a constant talker is difficult for a number of reasons: A) It's hard to keep them focused on the information you need. Each new question you ask inspires them to share another story, taking you farther and farther away from completing the phone call; B) It feels impossible to end the call politely, so you often stay on the call much longer than necessary, and sometimes end up responding with impatience or frustration, offending your customer; and C) The extended conversation can be exhausting, which then impacts your ability to provide excellent service to other customers.

So what can you do? How can you provide polite and professional customer service to a constant talker, keep that call short and still get all the information you need?

The answer is simple. Use their name!

We all respond to our names. When someone calls out our name we stop, look and listen. It is universal and it works every time. By using the constant talker's name, you will create a small space in the conversation in which you can refocus their thoughts or complete the call.

For example, let's say your customer David is describing, in specific detail, what happened on the day that his basement flooded. He's including when the storm started and where he was and what he was doing at the time and what the neighbours were doing and…you get the idea. In a gentle but clear tone of voice simply say his name —"*David*".

He will stop talking. There will be a brief bit of space before he says "*Yes?*" and at this moment you can redirect the conversation, ask your next question: "*It was a crazy storm that day. How much water came into your basement?*" You will likely have to do this several times in order to get all the details you need, but every time you say his name, David will stop talking and you'll be able to get him focused on your next question.

Once you get all the details you need, David may still keep talking. Now you can use his name to create the space you need to end the call. *"David…thanks so much for providing all these details today. It's always a pleasure speaking with you. Know that I will get back to you with the information you need no later than tomorrow morning. I do apologize but right now I must take another call* (or run to a meeting or speak to someone in your office). *Thanks again for giving me all these details and you'll hear from me very soon. I am ending our call. Bye for now."* And hang up.

This technique will not be comfortable the first time you use it. In fact, I encourage you to try it on family members or friends first, so you can experience its effectiveness. While they are sharing a story with you, simply say their name in a clear and friendly way. They will stop talking and create a moment of silence.

This technique is easier to use when refocusing a conversation than ending a call, but it does work. It is important to remember that staying on a lengthy, unproductive phone call limits your ability to provide excellent service to other customers. By keeping your voice friendly and clear, using words like *thank you* and *sorry,* and helping them visualize why you must end the call, you can maintain your reputation for great customer service while avoiding frustration and exhaustion.

When I apologize to an upset customer, I include an open-ended question. This is what I say:

_____

_____

_____

_____

_____

I can interrupt a constant talked by
using their name to create a moment
of silence.
I have practiced this technique on:

✓

_____

_____

_____

_____

_____

Did you know?

Voice mail was the brainchild of Gordon Mathews, a successful entrepreneur who held 35 US and foreign patents at the time of his death on February 23, 2002.

In the late seventies Matthews began working on the technology that would eventually be called "voicemail." In 1979, Matthews took this technology and formed a company called VMX, which stands for Voice Message Express. He applied for a patent in 1979 to cover his voicemail invention and sold the first system to 3M. A few years later, in 1982 the patent for his invention was awarded. His "Voice Message Exchange" managed electronic messages in a digital format. (As a side note: Mathews' wife, Monika, recorded the first greeting on this first commercial voicemail.)

From:
http://www.everyvoicemail.com/vm-resources.htm

13 *Telephone Elephants*

The phrase "the elephant in the room", widely attributed to Mark Twain, refers to an obvious truth or problem that is being ignored or which no one is willing to discuss openly.

When it comes to successful telephone communication, there are two such "elephants" (or "telephants" as one workshop participant suggested) that are important to acknowledge and explore.

The first is accents. Encountering an unfamiliar accent (or speech impediment) on the phone can be extremely intimidating. Many people get so nervous they end the call without any communication taking place. There is a way to prevent this from happening to you.

In the small town where I grew up, there weren't very many challenging accents — French, Italian, some Ukrainian. Or perhaps it was because I grew up with them that I didn't find them challenging. But when I moved to the very large city of Toronto, I realized that if I didn't figure out how to hear and understand a wide range of accents, I would encounter difficulties in stores, restaurants and my career.

Here's what I learned — accents are like music and you need to give yourself time to develop an ear for each accent, just as you would for new genres of music.

The biggest mistake we make is pressuring ourselves to understand an accent the moment we hear it. It's quite silly really. Why, if you've never heard a Mandarin or Newfoundland accent before, would you believe you should understand it immediately?

Like learning to appreciate a new genre of music—opera, blues, jazz, country, rap—you need time to begin recognizing certain sounds, patterns, nuances.

How do you create that time? You ask for it.

When you encounter an accent on the phone (or in person) that you don't understand, you need to say something. Here's what I recommend:

"I'm sorry but I am unfamiliar with your accent. I'm wondering if you can speak a bit slower and if you can repeat what you just said."

Why does this work? Well first of all, you aren't "blaming" the other person for your inability to communicate; you are taking full responsibility for creating great communication. Second, you are saying, very clearly, that you **want** to communicate, indicating both your respect and desire to speak with the other person. You are extending your hand to create relationship.

On the other end of the phone, what you will most often hear is a sigh of relief. Trust me, the person with the accent or speech impediment has endured many non-communicative phone conversations. They will be pleased that you are both willing and interested in speaking with them.

And what if you have the accent or speech impediment? At the beginning of the conversation, after you introduce yourself, simply say: *"I realize you may not be familiar with my accent. Let me know if you ever need me to repeat something or if you'd like me to speak more slowly."*

The second telephant we all need to consider is background noise, especially because our cellphones give us the ability to have conversations anytime, anywhere.

Know that all phones have microphones. Whatever the noise is around you, it will be louder to the person on the other end. There is very little you can do to prevent this from happening.

And the noise will be a constant distraction—unless you talk about it. Know that if you ignore the noise and keep talking, the other person will be thinking "What's that noise?" and hear very little of what you are saying.

As an example, for many years *The Phone Lady* shared office space with both a software company and a naval engineering firm. There were several people in these organizations that brought their dogs to work and I enjoyed having gentle and affectionate pets come by to visit throughout the day. But one of the dogs, Tiller, got a bit blind and deaf with age and took to... spontaneous barking.

During this time I was working on a project for a client scheduling appointments with CEOs of gold mining companies on Bay Street in Toronto. No matter how carefully I timed the call, eventually I would be in conversation with a CEO and Tiller would start barking.

Now, if I ignored the noise, I would automatically tense up a bit, wondering if the CEO had heard the barking and, if so, what he/she was thinking. And, on the other end, the sound of the barking would cause the CEO to take my call less seriously, make him/her visualize me running some sort of telephone scam from my basement. The noise would distract them for the remainder of the call and very little communication would take place.

So, as soon as possible after Tiller barked I would say: *"So sorry about that. I work in an office where people bring their dogs to work and that was Tiller."*

The first response was always: *"You work in an office where people bring their dogs to work. How fun is that!"*

And then they would ask: *"What kind of a dog is Tiller?"*

"He's a golden retriever," I'd reply.

"Oh," they'd say. *"I love golden retrievers."* And we'd have a brief conversation about dogs and how wonderful they are as pets and companions.

What's most interesting is each CEO that experienced the barking, and the visual I provided when it happened, booked an appointment with my client. Why? Because we moved from being two strangers sharing words on the phone into true communication.

When there is noise around you, use your words to create a visual for the other person. If you work in a busy office, you might say *"There's lots of activity in our office today, so that's what you are hearing in the background."* Or if you take a call while in a crowded public space, like a mall or grocery store, you might say *"You've reached me in a store that's quite noisy but I am moving to a quieter spot."* Use your words to put the other person at ease and refocus them on the conversation instead of the noise.

And when there's noise on the caller's end that distracts you, mention it. Here are some examples:

"It sounds like you're driving your car."

"It sounds like you've got energetic children at home today."

"It sounds like you're in a meeting."

One more story:

I rarely take on projects that involve calling people at home, but when a friend asked, I agreed to be involved. On one of the calls a woman answered the phone and her television was on so loudly behind her I knew there was no way we were going to be able to have a conversation. I happened to look at the time and then said *"Are you watching Dr. Phil?"*

"Yes", she said.

"Okay. Should I call back when it's over?"

"No," she said. *"It's a repeat."* And she went, turned down the sound and returned to the phone ready to talk with me.

In order to create conversation, you must acknowledge those things that will prevent communication from taking place. Use your words and create visual images that eliminate distractions and inspire curiosity.

Try these techniques during the coming weeks and months. Stay present to how they enhance your ability to communicate on the phone and share your experiences with others.

Did you know?

In the 1960's the American television comedy "Get Smart" introduced the concept of a shoe phone. Although the technology probably didn't exist at the time, the CIA put one of fictional secret agent Maxwell Smart's prop shoe phones on exhibit in their museum. Nevertheless the famous shoe phone is often credited as one of the earliest Wi-Fi communication devices. Similarly, many people believe (mistakenly) that the popular flip phone was based on the transponder used by the actors in the original sci-fi series "Star Trek".

And turning the clock back a few more decades, the comic strip detective Dick Tracy wore a two-way radio wristwatch. This was one idea that really caught on. Today smartwatches can do just about anything—play music, show videos, accept long-distance telephone calls and of course, tell time.

Should I Cold Call?

14

There are a lot of sales pundits out there loudly proclaiming that "the cold call is dead". It isn't necessary any more, they say. We can use social media and email and other technology-based tools to reach our prospects. We don't need to phone them.

This isn't true. There are a lot of reasons why cold calling should be an essential part of a company's sales and marketing efforts. But before I get into those details, it's important that we have the same definition of cold calling.

The phrase comes from the notion that you are calling someone "cold", i.e. you don't know them, you've never spoken to them before, they are not expecting your call, they are unfamiliar with your company, etc. It is also widely associated with selling— fast, tough and greedy selling. And this is why so many people believe they should avoid it at all costs.

So the first thing I want to share is my belief that cold calling isn't about selling. It's about introducing yourself, your product, your service to your potential customers and clients. It's a vital part of completing your research on these potential clients... before you begin the sales process.

The word "prospecting" is more attractive and palatable than "cold calling". As a native of a northern gold mining community, I have a cherished affinity for this word. I knew several "old time" prospectors growing up, men that went deep into the bush and panned for gold. And there are a lot of similarities between this activity and how we build a client list.(Mind you, I'm forever grateful that I prospect from my lovely, yellow and green office surrounded by trees rather than in a canvas tent eating cold beans and surrounded by black flies.)

I encourage you to replace the phrase "cold calling" with "prospecting" and know that prospecting is not about selling; it is about learning more about your prospective customers and verifying that your product or service is of value to them.

Whether you are building your business by contacting people you already know, or dealing strictly with referrals, or reaching out to people based on a job title or industry sector, you must first find out more about them and their needs. Here's an example of what I mean:

A person calls me to sell photocopier toner. There's an assumption made that because I'm a business owner I have a photocopier in my office. Well, I don't. So for me this is a pretty fast call. "Sorry," I say, "I don't own a photocopier." And that's the end of the call.

Now if that same person called me and actually introduced themselves and their company and moved to asking me a few questions about my business (most people are proud of their businesses and are pleased to answer a question or two by someone who displays a true interest) then they would know pretty quickly that I'm not a candidate for toner. But maybe I'm a potential customer for another product line. Or maybe I'm planning to purchase a photocopier in a year's time, so they could call back then. Or maybe I can be removed from the potential customer list altogether, freeing up time and energy for other calls.

Prospecting is quite simply the last, and most important, step in your research process. Through your phone call to a prospect you will determine if you can fill a need or solve a problem for them. When the answer is "yes" then you can organize a meeting or send along information and begin the sales process.

Certainly there are businesses that do not need to prospect in this way. In some cases, all potential clients can be met with face-to-face, through networking, conferences, trade shows, etc. And there are companies that can reach desired revenue by marketing a product through social media channels and email campaigns. So, how do you know if you need to pick up the phone?

Here's a simple formula I use all the time with my clients and it produces great (and incredibly accurate) results:

Step One

Figure out the average revenue of one of your average clients for one year.

For example, if you own a spa, an average client might use your services 10 times each year and spend $150 per visit. This would give you an average revenue figure of $1,500 per client.

Or let's say you're a Realtor. The mid-range selling price of a home in your market could be $350,000 and you might earn a 2.5% commission on that sale. This would give you an average revenue figure of $8,750 per client.

In both examples there would be clients that would spend much less—and clients that would spend much more. You want to settle on an <u>average</u> revenue figure.

Step Two

What is your revenue goal for the next twelve months?

Very simple—do you want this to be an $80,000 year, a $150,000 year, a $500,000 year?

Step Three

Divide your answer from Step One (average annual revenue of one average client) into your answer from Step Two (your revenue goal). The answer is the number of average clients you need in the next twelve months to reach your goal.

For example, if the spa owner wants to generate $80,000 in revenue, she will need 53 average clients. If she wants to make $150,000, she will need 100 average clients, and if she wants to generate $500,000, she will need 333 average clients.

For the Realtor the numbers are 9 average clients for $80,000, 11 to 12 average clients for $100,000 and 57 average clients for $500,000.

Multiply your answer in Step 3 by 10. Why? Because an average salesperson (and I do realize you may be well above average; in fact, since you're reading this book, that's probably the case) gains a new client once out of every 10 prospects they pitch.

So, for the spa owner, she needs to reach 530, 1,000 or 3,330 potential clients respectively. For the Realtor, the numbers are 90, 120 or 570 average clients.

The larger the number in Step Four, the more you need to include prospecting into your sales and marketing plans.

Here's how it breaks down:

1   If the spa owner is aiming for $80,000 in revenue, she would take her final number and divide it by 12 (for the months of the year). So the spa owner needs to introduce her services to 530/12 = 44 new prospects each month. Connecting with this many qualified prospects a month cannot be accomplished by networking or trade shows alone.

2   If the Realtor is aiming for $80,000 in revenue, they need to introduce their services to 90/12= 7.5 monthly. Connecting with 7.5 qualified leads a month can be accomplished through networking and community activities so, in this case, the Realtor does not need to include phone prospecting in their sales and marketing plans.

Sometimes this formula can indicate that prices need to increase, or that you need to focus on selling differently. For example, in order for the spa owner to generate $500,000, she needs to reach 3,330 prospects, which would mean 277.5 conversations with prospects each month. That's a full-time job on the phone for two people! The spa owner can look at the pricing structure in order to increase the average worth of an average customer or perhaps organize packages for bridal parties, corporate events, birthday celebrations, etc. Each sale of a package would bring multiple prospects into the spa and experiencing the spa's treatments would be the best form of advertising.

If the Realtor wants to generate $500,000, they need to reach 570 prospects or 47.5 per month. Again, this is too big a number to accomplish by networking alone, but when we break the number down further (divide by 48 to create a weekly goal), the Realtor needs to have 12 conversations each week. That's something that can be done by phone with a commitment of approximately three hours a week. And the Realtor could look at organizing workshops for first-time buyers or holding a community event in a neighbourhood where they have multiple listings.

While prospecting by phone has definitely changed, and will definitely keep changing along with our phones and the technology we have available, it remains an important and viable way to grow a business and increase revenue.

Should I Prospect on the Phone?

1. The average annual worth of one client for me is:

_____

_____

_____

_____

_____

2. In the next 12 months, I want to create this much revenue: ✓

_____

_____

_____

_____

_____

3. By dividing my average annual worth of one client into my desired revenue, I discover I need this many average clients: ✓

_____

_____

_____

_____

_____

4. I multiply the average number of clients I need by 10 and discover how many people I need to introduce to my service or product:

✓

_____

_____

_____

_____

_____

Did you know?

Born in 1930 and raised on a busy farm in rural Nova Scotia, my mother-in-law, Norma Potter, first knew the telephone to be a "party line". Party lines were local phone circuits that provided service to multiple subscribers. They were not only less expensive for customers, but during wartime shortages of metals such as copper, they were often all that was available. A shared phone line meant no privacy and was often the source of both news and gossip.

As a little girl, Norma overheard a conversation about someone's death or impending death. Such important news was too difficult to keep to herself and she shared it when visiting the neighbours. Unfortunately she got it wrong. She can't remember if she repeated that someone died when they hadn't, or if indeed someone died, but she got the name wrong. In any case, she was punished by her parents for both listening in on the phone call and repeating what she heard. To this day she is uncomfortable on the telephone and she never gossips.

Review Notes

15 *What's Next*

While a friend was staying with me as part of a business trip recently, his sister-in-law, in hospital in Europe and surrounded by family, made the decision to be disconnected from dialysis. It was a life-ending decision for her and a life-altering decision for my friend and his partner of 30 years.

I couldn't help but overhear parts of their conversation on the phone that day, how it included all the words and tones of compassion, support and grief. Sharing tears on the phone is an act of intimacy that contains a rare depth of love and connection. It cannot be duplicated with any other medium.

While this is a very personal and emotional example of phone communication, it succinctly illustrates my belief that speaking to each other on the phone will always hold value.

It will, of course, continue to change—has changed immensely even in the last two years. Businesses thrive without landlines, it's no longer rude to not return every call we receive, all of us answer our phones less often and even the word "phone" encompasses everything from photographs and videos to social media and fitness statistics.

But despite all this change, the phone call remains a vital component of successful business relationships. Today, television business programs include entrepreneurs that are continually challenged about their phone behaviour. Questions and instructions often include: "Have you called...?"; "Why didn't you pick up the phone?"; "I can make that connection with one phone call."; and "We need to get on the phone."

From customer service to accounts receivable and from job search to prospecting, a phone conversation remains the most direct, efficient and cost-effective way to both hear and engage others. Messages on a screen do not build relationship, inspire conversation, uncover an impactful backstory or reveal unexpected opportunities.

Which brings me to Marshall McLuhan.

Fifty years ago, this Alberta-born Canadian published a book called Understanding Media: The Extensions of Man. Within its pages he released the idea **"The medium is the message."**

This all happened on the periphery of my life. I was five years old when Understanding Media was published yet I had already absorbed its main premise, that **"a medium is not something neutral, it does something to people"**. I understood this because of my mother.

The home I grew up in had a family room that was an addition to the original structure. The kitchen window, that once looked out over the backyard, was left in place and provided my mom a great way to keep an eye on me. It also gave me the ability to eavesdrop on her.

We lived in Northern Ontario, far away from my mom's family and many of her friends. But even the friends that lived nearby had their hands full with growing families - or were housebound by harsh winter weather. The phone in the kitchen was my mother's lifeline and its "ring ring" or the sound of the rotary dial was, for me, an overture to theatre.

Her listening and laughing, the story telling and offered advice, her organizing of events and meetings—and sometimes the tears and frustration—became the background music of my pre-school years, and made me believe that the telephone had a powerful magic.

I still do believe that—well, maybe not the magic part. But what I've come to understand, as I've moved through a career that's included typewriters and Dictaphones, Dewey Decimal and microfiche, smart phones and 3D printers, is McLuhan's theory holds true—**"...people are changed by the instruments they employ."**

For me, the change that occurs when we pick up the phone and speak to each other, rather than click away on our keyboards, is incredibly powerful and vital.

For example, I recently had a 30-minute conversation with a potential new client. Prior to that conversation we had connected through social media, each of us likely taking cursory glances at the other's profile. Then we used email to pinpoint a time in our busy schedules for the phone conversation, and while this was happening, I went and explored the company's website. None of these mediums prepared me for what happened next.

The phone call started out as many do. At his request, I described my work and provided examples of what I teach. He agreed with everything I said and his voice changed as he became more interested and, as he later revealed, inspired. By the time I quoted him a price on workshops he, being the ultimate entrepreneur, had moved well past that idea into something more proactive, detailed and valuable for him and his team— and for me.

In fact, this one phone call has brought me several unexpected and important business relationships and it continues to impact the growth and success of *The Phone Lady*.

What happened in this call could not have happened in the black and white and pause of email or texting because it happened in the sound of our voices, in the real time exchange of ideas, in the discovery of common ground and the possibility of partnership.

And while this could have happened face-to-face, there would have been tremendous time delays and expense. Instead, the phone allowed us to discover each other—and change each other—from a distance of 3,000 miles.

All of the mediums we use to communicate with each other have value. And, just as McLuhan revealed all those years ago, **the medium we choose influences how the message is received**. As a choice, the phone's power lies in its ability to expose our thoughts and feelings in real time, to move past basic facts and data into the realm of ideas and, more importantly, into relationship.

A phone call says we are interested and open—in you, the customer—in you, the possible employer—in you, the potential client.

Does the future hold more and more people using the phone less and less as a means of conversation? Yes, I believe so. Since I delivered my first phone communication workshop in 2006,

I've witnessed a steady increase in the number of people, of all ages, who are uncomfortable, nervous or afraid of speaking on the phone.

Young people can be the most intimidated by phone conversations, a natural consequence of what they've seen and learned from their elders. While I grew up constantly listening to adults on the phone, many people under the age of 25 grew up witnessing only text and email activity. They simply haven't been exposed to the skill set enough to understand its value.

And I predict that this will create unexpected opportunities for those who are willing to develop their phone communication skills.

Companies committed to building and maintaining strong relationships will not be satisfied with text-only communication. They will choose to employ those who know how to speak on the phone, people who can create conversation and hear what's being said. Those with proficiency in phone communication will be sought after and offered possibilities unavailable to those who've limited themselves to text on a screen.

Will continuing advances and changes in equipment impact phone communication?

Most certainly. A day will arrive when the majority of phone calls will include real time video interaction. This will impact some of the skills reviewed in this book and force us to cultivate new ones in order to master different communication challenges.

It's also possible that phones, the equipment we use to speak to each other, will become smaller, perhaps worn on our clothing like the communicator badges on several of the Star Trek series.

But the phone is not going to disappear.

Its fate is not the same as the VCR or tape recorder. It has not been replaced by a new way of doing things. Instead it has proliferated and expanded its usefulness.

Phone calls may indeed decline but for those that can dial and speak, it will be as if they wield a super power when it comes to building businesses, growing relationships and getting things done.

So, if you've chosen to read this last chapter first, I encourage you to start at the beginning, to learn the skills, wield the power. And keep an eye on *The Phone Lady* and the introduction of new ways to learn, develop and excel at phone communication.

Acknowledgements

First and foremost thanks to my friend and publisher, Douglas Arthur Brown. Without his enthusiasm, encouragement and cheerleading this book would still be an idea. My stepdaughter Natasha Marchewka, who saw this book in my future long before I did — and kept reminding me. My husband, David Potter, for running errands, giving me the time and space to focus, keeping me calm and always making me laugh. Lise Noël, Manager of the Bell Historical Collection, a marvelous resource who answered many questions and sent many packages. Finally, tremendous thanks to Halifax, to Nova Scotia and to every client, colleague and contact that I've met and worked with since 2006. You have inspired this book and allowed *The Phone Lady* to thrive.